I0448387

April 9, 2014

The Honorable Randy Neugebauer
Chairman
Subcommittee on Housing and Insurance
Committee on Financial Services
House of Representatives

Overview of GAO's Past Work on the National Flood Insurance Program

Dear Mr. Chairman:

Floods are the most common and destructive natural disaster in the United States. The National Flood Insurance Program (NFIP), which collected about $3.8 billion in premiums and insured about $1.3 trillion in property in 2013, is administered by the Federal Emergency Management Agency (FEMA). The program is a key component of the federal government's efforts to limit the damage and financial impact of floods. NFIP makes federally backed flood insurance available to property owners in participating communities. Additionally, through NFIP, FEMA maps floodplain boundaries, and requires participating communities to adopt and enforce floodplain management regulations that mitigate the effects of flooding.

The program has faced significant ongoing financial and management challenges over the years. In particular, the program is unlikely to generate sufficient revenue to cover future catastrophic losses or repay billions of dollars borrowed from the Department of the Treasury (Treasury) to cover insurance claims from previous disasters. As a result, the program has been on GAO's High-Risk List since 2006.[1]

In July 2012, Congress enacted the Biggert-Waters Flood Insurance Reform Act of 2012 (Biggert-Waters Act), which contained provisions to help strengthen the future financial solvency and administrative efficiency of NFIP. The Biggert-Waters Act affected many aspects of NFIP. For example, it required FEMA to phase out almost all discounted insurance premiums (commonly referred to as subsidized premiums), establish a reserve fund, improve flood risk mapping, and develop new methods related to compensation for the companies that sell and service flood insurance policies.[2] On March 21, 2014, Congress enacted the Homeowner Flood Insurance Affordability Act of 2014 (2014 Act), which repeals or alters portions of the Biggert-Waters Act.[3] For example, the 2014 Act (1) permits certain premium subsidies removed by the

---

[1]Every 2 years, we provide Congress with an update on our High-Risk Program, which highlights major areas that are at high risk for fraud, waste, abuse, or mismanagement, or need broad reform. See GAO, *High-Risk Series: An Update,* GAO-13-283 (Washington, D.C.: Feb. 14, 2013).

[2]The Biggert-Waters Act left in place subsidies for a limited set of properties, including those behind certain unfinished or decertified levees and those in communities that are in the process of joining NFIP and therefore part of NFIP's emergency program.

[3]Homeowner Flood Insurance Affordability Act of 2014, Pub. L. No. 113-89 (Mar. 21, 2014).

Biggert-Waters Act for properties not insured by NFIP as of July 6, 2012, and for properties purchased after July 6, 2012; (2) restores grandfathered rates (that is, rates that were not changed after properties were remapped into higher-risk flood zones) removed by the Biggert-Waters Act, effective retroactively to the Biggert-Waters Act's enactment on July 6, 2012; (3) generally limits yearly increases in property-specific premium rates to 18 percent; (4) requires annual premium increases of at least 5 percent for certain subsidized policies; and (5) generally adds an annual surcharge of $25 for residential properties and $250 for nonresidential properties and secondary residences. Because the 2014 Act was enacted shortly before our publication date, this report does not fully address its impact on FEMA's activities. However, we describe key provisions in the 2014 act that relate to the issues discussed in this report. We plan to include information and analysis regarding FEMA's implementation of the 2014 Act in future work on NFIP.

To help Congress monitor and consider the future of NFIP, you asked us to provide an overview of the key challenges facing the program. This report summarizes our prior work on issues facing the program and provides an update on the status of these issues.

Scope and Methodology

This report summarizes prior work from April 2003 through February 2014 in the following areas: (1) finances, (2) premium rate setting, (3) community and property owner participation, (4) flood mapping, (5) flood mitigation, (6) administration and oversight, and (7) information management. Where relevant, we also discuss program changes required by the Biggert-Waters Act and the 2014 Act.

To conduct this work, we reviewed reports we issued about NFIP from April 2003 through February 2014. For a list of these and related reports, see "Related GAO Products" at the end of this report. Also, please see the scope and methodology for each of these reports for details on how we conducted that work. We also reviewed documentation from FEMA and interviewed FEMA officials on the status of our prior recommendations as well as FEMA's efforts to implement requirements in the Biggert-Waters Act. In addition, we reviewed the 2014 Act and identified provisions that repealed or altered Biggert-Waters Act requirements. Where appropriate, we obtained other FEMA documents and data to update our prior work and provide current information on NFIP. Enclosure VIII provides the status of our recent audit recommendations concerning NFIP. We also analyzed FEMA policy data as of the end of fiscal year 2013 to update program statistics and calculate progress in building a reserve fund. Additionally, we analyzed policy and claims data from calendar years 2010 and 2012 to provide perspective on the magnitude of payments to private insurance companies that sell and service NFIP policies. We assessed the reliability of these data by conducting electronic testing and interviewing FEMA officials. We determined that the data were sufficiently reliable for purposes of describing key aspects of NFIP's financial status and business activity.

We performed the work on which this report was based in accordance with generally accepted government auditing standards. Those standards require that we plan and perform the audit to obtain sufficient, appropriate evidence to provide a reasonable basis for our findings and conclusions based on our audit objectives. We believe the evidence obtained provides a reasonable basis for our findings and conclusions based on our audit objectives.

Results in Brief

Over the past 11 years, we have identified a variety of challenges facing NFIP and have made numerous recommendations to FEMA to improve its administration of the program. FEMA has generally agreed with our recommendations and has taken steps to implement them. However, FEMA has not fully addressed all of the issues we have reported on and will need to address provisions in both the Biggert-Waters Act and the 2014 Act that affect many aspects of NFIP, including its finances, rate setting, mapping, and participation, among other things. The 2014 Act includes provisions that address affordability concerns for affected property owners. However, these provisions may also reduce program revenues and weaken the potential for improved financial soundness of the NFIP program.

Background

The National Flood Insurance Act of 1968 established NFIP as an alternative to providing direct disaster relief after floods and was intended to reduce the federal government's escalating costs for repairing flood damage after disasters.[4] According to NFIP statistics, 90 percent of all national disasters in the United States have involved flooding. However, flooding is generally excluded from homeowners' policies that typically cover damages from other losses, such as wind, fire, and theft. Because of the catastrophic nature of flooding and the inability to adequately predict flood risks, historically, private insurance companies have largely been unwilling to underwrite and bear the risk that results from providing primary flood insurance coverage.

As of May 2013, about 22,000 communities across the United States and its territories voluntarily participated in NFIP by adopting and agreeing to enforce flood-related building codes and floodplain management regulations to reduce future flood damage. In exchange, NFIP makes federally backed flood insurance available to homeowners and other property owners (for example, businesses, churches, and farmers) in these communities. Homeowners with mortgages held by federally regulated lenders on property in participating communities identified by FEMA to be in special flood hazard areas (SFHA) are required to purchase flood insurance (mandatory purchase requirement).

As shown in table 1, NFIP coverage limits vary by program (regular or emergency) and property type (for example, residential or nonresidential).[5] In NFIP's regular program, the maximum coverage limits for residential policyholders are $250,000 for buildings and $100,000 for contents. The 2014 Act permits residential policyholders to forego coverage for detached structures that are part of residential property but that do not serve as residences.[6] For commercial policyholders (that is, those with policies for nonresidential properties), the maximum coverage limit is $500,000 per building and $500,000 for contents owned by the building owner. There is additional coverage for contents owned by the tenants.

---

[4]Pub. L. No. 90-448, Title XIII, § 1301 et seq., 82 Stat. 476, 576 (1968).

[5]NFIP's emergency program is limited to communities that are in the process of joining NFIP.

[6]Pub. L. No. 113-89, § 13.

Table 1: NFIP Coverage Limits, as of January 2014

	Regular program			Emergency program[a]
Building coverage[b]	Basic limit	Additional limit	Total limit	Total limit
One- to four-unit residential	$60,000	$190,000	$250,000	$35,000
Other residential	175,000	75,000	250,000	100,000
Nonresidential	175,000	325,000	500,000	100,000
Contents coverage[c]				
Residential	25,000	75,000	100,000	10,000
Nonresidential	150,000	350,000	500,000	100,000

Source: FEMA.

[a]NFIP's emergency program is limited to communities that are in the process of joining NFIP.

[b]Building coverage includes the replacement value of the building and its foundation, electrical and plumbing systems, central air and heating, furnaces and water heaters, and equipment considered part of the overall structure of the building.

[c]Contents coverage includes items such as clothing, furniture, and portable electronic equipment.

NFIP differentiates two levels of coverage under the regular program—basic and additional. Because claims are more likely to be made against the first several thousand dollars of coverage than against higher levels of coverage, FEMA charges a higher insurance premium per $100 of basic coverage than it does per $100 of additional coverage.[7]

Congress and FEMA intended that, insofar as practicable, NFIP be funded with premiums collected from policyholders. However, the program, by design, is not actuarially sound because Congress has historically authorized FEMA to offer subsidized premium rates for policies covering certain structures to encourage prospective customers who might become insured to join the program. As a result, NFIP has not been able to generate sufficient premiums to cover losses and other program costs, and FEMA has needed to borrow money from Treasury to pay for claims in some years.[8]

FEMA charges full-risk rates (that is, rates intended to reflect the actual risk of flooding) and rates that are less than full risk. Properties that are not charged property-specific full-risk rates have included those with rates that were not changed (grandfathered) after being remapped into higher-risk flood zones, as well as those with subsidized rates.[9] The largest number of

---

[7]For perspective, the basic residential coverage under the regular program is $60,000, and the average residential flood claim from 2007 through 2012 was about $31,000.

[8]FEMA has authority to borrow money from Treasury to pay losses that exceed premium revenue and any accumulated surplus.

[9]FEMA does not categorize policies with grandfathered rates as "subsidized" because they are within classes of policies that are not subsidized for the class as a whole. However, FEMA officials acknowledged that property owners that obtain grandfathered rates are being cross-subsidized by other policyholders in the same flood zone that are paying higher rates.

subsidized policies is for properties built before Flood Insurance Rate Maps (FIRM) became available (pre-FIRM policies).[10]

NFIP is managed by FEMA's Federal Insurance and Mitigation Administration (FIMA), with administrative support from FEMA's Mission Support Bureau. FEMA is housed within the Department of Homeland Security (DHS), which provides FEMA with management direction by issuing guidance and working to integrate its various management processes, systems, and staff within and across its management areas. About 390 FEMA employees manage and oversee NFIP and the National Flood Insurance Fund, into which premiums are deposited and from which claims and expenses are paid. FIMA staff are responsible for monitoring and overseeing the performance of private insurers who participate in the Write-Your-Own (WYO) program—the primary means of selling and servicing NFIP policies—to help ensure that NFIP is administered properly. FEMA also relies on contractors to administer key aspects of the program. For example, contractors collect NFIP data, market the program, and help map flood hazards.

Findings

In summary, we found the following:

- *Finances.* As of December 31, 2013, FEMA owed Treasury $24 billion—primarily to pay claims associated with Superstorm Sandy (2012) and Hurricane Katrina (2005)—and had not made a principal payment since 2010 (see enclosure I). The Biggert-Waters Act requires FEMA to issue a report to Congress by January 2013 on a repayment plan setting forth options to repay FEMA's total debt to Treasury within 10 years.[11] However, as of January 2014, FEMA had not issued such a report. According to FEMA officials, preliminary analysis suggests that, under FEMA's planned implementation of the act, the agency will not be able to repay its debt within the 10-year time frame. The officials said the report will contain options for retiring the debt within 10 years, but that most of the options would require congressional action. Additionally, while FEMA is establishing a reserve fund as required by the act, it is unlikely to initially meet the act's annual targets for building up the reserve, due partly to statutory limitations on annual premium increases. Further, the reasonableness of FEMA's compensation to WYO companies remains unclear because FEMA has not fully addressed our 2009 recommendations to provide transparency and accountability of its payments to WYOs.

- *Premium rate setting.* FEMA's methodology for determining full-risk premium rates may not fully reflect the actual risk of flood damage, adding to concerns about NFIP's financial stability (see enclosure II). Consistent with recommendations we made in 2008, FEMA has initiated actions to improve the accuracy of full-risk rates, including updating data used in its rate-setting model. However, these actions are in the preliminary stages. FEMA had also begun implementing Biggert-Waters Act provisions to reduce and eventually eliminate most subsidized rates on remaining policies. However, the 2014 Act reinstates some of these

---

[10]FEMA also subsidizes policies for properties—for example, properties behind certain unfinished or decertified levees, certain post-FIRM properties, and emergency program properties are subsidized.

[11]Pub. L. No. 112-141, § 100213,126 Stat. 405, 925 (2012). Additionally, after borrowing funds, FEMA must report to Congress and Treasury on the 6-month anniversary and every 6 months thereafter on the progress of the repayment. Id. § 100213(a).

subsidies. Phasing out and eventually eliminating subsidies remaining after the 2014 Act poses challenges for FEMA. For example, to appropriately revise rates for previously subsidized policies, FEMA will need information on the relative risk of flooding and property elevations that generally had not been required for subsidized policies prior to the Biggert-Waters Act. FEMA is evaluating approaches to obtain this information in response to a recommendation we made in a 2013 report. Premium rate increases remaining in effect after the 2014 Act may also pose affordability challenges for some homeowners, particularly those with low or moderate incomes. The 2014 Act's repeal of certain rate increases in the Biggert-Waters Act will address affordability concerns for affected property owners. But the repeal may also reduce program revenues and weaken the potential for improved financial soundness of NFIP, and will likely prolong the program's long-term burden on taxpayers.

- *Participation.* Nationwide NFIP penetration rates—the proportion of all properties with flood insurance—are low, according to estimates based on available limited data (see enclosure III). In addition, information on the extent of compliance with the mandatory purchase requirement is limited. As of September 31, 2013, there were more than 5.5 million NFIP policies in force, but several factors have negatively affected program participation. These include inaccurate perceptions about the risk of flooding and the cost of purchasing policies, as well as inaccurate assumptions that flood perils are included in homeowners insurance policies. FEMA has taken a number of steps to broaden participation in NFIP, including development of a national outreach strategy. In addition, the Biggert-Waters Act included several provisions to strengthen enforcement of the mandatory purchase requirement and along with the 2014 Act addresses some of the factors that limit participation.

- *Flood mapping.* FEMA has taken steps to enhance the accuracy of flood maps and must address new requirements regarding map accuracy (see enclosure IV). FEMA is responsible for flood mapping activities and develops flood mapping policy and guidance. Accurate and updated flood hazard maps are important because without them, property owners could underestimate their exposure to flood risks and make poor financial decisions about protecting their properties. FEMA has taken steps to increase map accuracy, for example by establishing standards for the quality of data used to develop new flood maps. The Biggert-Waters Act authorized several statutory changes to further improve the accuracy of flood maps, including creation of an expert council to advise FEMA on incorporating the best available climate science in flood maps and using the best available methodology to consider the impact of rising sea levels and future development on flood risk. Additionally, the 2014 Act requires FEMA to implement a flood mapping program, after review by the expert council, that results in technically credible flood hazard data in all areas for which flood maps are prepared or updated.

- *Flood mitigation.* FEMA supports a variety of flood mitigation activities that are designed to reduce flood risk and the financial exposure of NFIP (see enclosure V). FEMA's mitigation programs fund activities such as local hazard mitigation planning, natural protective features such as wetlands, and property-level mitigation efforts such as elevating buildings. These programs generally have a nonfederal cost-sharing requirement. Communities play a key role in mitigating flood risk through planning and enforcement. For example, when communities join NFIP, they must enforce flood-related building codes, including those regulating where structures may be built within the floodplain. In July 2013, we concluded that one option for reducing flood risk and financial exposure would be for FEMA to increase its mitigation efforts. However, the cost of mitigation can be high, and the demand for mitigation funds currently exceeds appropriated amounts.

- *Administration and oversight.* FEMA faces ongoing challenges in key administrative and oversight functions (see enclosure VI). For example, FEMA does not have a strategic human capital plan that meets statutory requirements. FEMA has started to develop such a plan in response to a recommendation we made in 2011 but this plan is currently under management review. FEMA also has experienced problems in overseeing NFIP contractors but has made recent progress in this area. In addition, FEMA is in the process of addressing recommendations we made in 2009 and 2011 to strengthen acquisition management and controls over financial management and oversight.

- *Information management.* FEMA faces ongoing challenges in key information technology systems that support NFIP (see enclosure VII). For example, FEMA does not have a centralized document management system and has an outdated financial management system. Additionally, FEMA lacks a modern policy and claims management system despite investing significant time and resources. In 2011, we made recommendations designed to improve key aspects of FEMA's system development efforts. FEMA has taken some steps to address them, including clarifying system requirements and creating a process for identifying and mitigating project risks. FEMA must follow through on these steps to ensure that its next flood insurance policy and claims processing system fully supports mission needs.

Agency Comments

We provided a draft of this report to DHS for its review and comment. DHS provided technical comments, which we incorporated, as appropriate.

As agreed with your offices, unless you publicly announce the contents of this report earlier, we plan no further distribution until 30 days from the report date. At that time, we will send copies to the Secretary of Homeland Security, relevant congressional committees, and other interested parties. In addition, the report will be available at no charge on GAO's website at http://www.gao.gov.

If you or your staff have any questions or wish to discuss the material in this report further, please contact me at (202) 512-8678 or garciadiazd@gao.gov. Contact points for our Offices of Congressional Relations and Public Affairs may be found on the last page of this report. GAO staff members who made major contributions to this report include Steve Westley, Assistant Director; Emily Chalmers; Karen Jarzynka-Hernandez; Lisa Moore; Frank Todisco; and Jessica Sandler.

Sincerely yours,

Daniel Garcia-Diaz
Director, Financial Markets and
    Community Investment

Enclosures-8

Enclosure I: Finances

Background

The Federal Emergency Management Agency (FEMA) funds the National Flood Insurance Program (NFIP) primarily through insurance premiums paid by policyholders but receives appropriations for some flood mapping and mitigation activities. NFIP premiums must cover insurance claims and all program costs, including outreach, research, and operating expenses. When premiums are insufficient to cover these costs, FEMA may borrow money from Treasury. Congress sets limits on the overall amount that FEMA may borrow (borrowing authority).

FEMA sells and services NFIP policies primarily through private insurance companies that participate in the Write-Your-Own (WYO) program. FEMA compensates the companies based on a percentage of premiums and claims.

Although FEMA performs many of the same activities as a private insurance company, because of statutory restrictions it cannot operate NFIP the way a private company can operate certain lines of business. For example, FEMA cannot refuse to insure high-risk properties, drop coverage on multiclaim policies, diversify risk, or immediately move to charging full-risk insurance premiums on all policies.

FEMA Owes $24 Billion to Treasury and Does Not Expect to Meet Repayment and Reserve Fund Targets

As of December 31, 2013, FEMA owed Treasury $24 billion, and its borrowing authority was $30.4 billion. FEMA's debt to Treasury stems from collecting insufficient premiums to cover claims and program costs. (See enclosure II for information on how FEMA sets premium rates.) Over the years, Congress has authorized increases in FEMA's borrowing authority in response to catastrophic storms. Prior to Hurricane Katrina in 2005, when FEMA borrowed from Treasury, Congress either retired the debt or FEMA repaid the loans, generally within 2 years.[12] FEMA's borrowing authority prior to Katrina was less than $2 billion. To allow FEMA to borrow sufficient amounts to pay claims associated with Hurricanes Katrina, Wilma, and Rita Congress increased FEMA's borrowing authority three times from September 2005 through March 2006 to over $20.7 billion. Most recently, Congress increased FEMA's borrowing authority by $9.7 billion in 2013, which allowed FEMA to borrow an additional $6.25 billion to pay claims associated with Superstorm Sandy, which occurred in 2012.

FEMA has made interest payments on its loans from Treasury but has not made principal payments since 2010. According to FEMA officials, in some years the agency has not had sufficient funds to make principal payments and, in other years, could have made principal payments but chose to preserve its cash balances to help avoid the need for future borrowing. FEMA has refinanced all of its Katrina-related debt with Treasury as the loans have reached their maturity dates. The refinancings have lowered FEMA's interest payments because interest rates have declined since the mid-2000s. For example, FEMA paid more than $730 million in interest for Katrina-related debt in 2008 and about $72 million in interest in 2011.[13] FEMA's

---

[12]Borrowings through 1985 were repaid from congressional appropriations. NFIP did not borrow from 1986 through 1993. Since 1994, FEMA has repaid loans from premium and other income.

[13]The reduction in the interest payment also reflects the fact that FEMA paid back about 10 percent (approximately $1.6 billion in principal) of its Katrina-related debt during that time frame.

largest outstanding loan of $16 billion matures in September 2014. Because FEMA does not have the ability to repay this amount, the loan will likely be refinanced at that time, according to FEMA officials.

Preliminary FEMA analysis from before the enactment of the 2014 Act suggests that the agency will not be able to repay its debt within the time frame set forth in the Biggert-Waters Act. The Biggert-Waters Act requires FEMA to issue a report to Congress setting forth options to repay FEMA's total debt to Treasury within 10 years.[14] Although the report was due in January 2013, FEMA had not issued such a report as of January 2014. FEMA officials told us they had drafted a report, which is currently undergoing management review, that assesses FEMA's repayment ability under scenarios that use different assumptions about future NFIP losses. The officials said the assessment showed that, under FEMA's planned implementation of the Biggert-Waters Act, the agency would not reach the 10-year repayment goal under any of the scenarios. The officials said the report will contain options for retiring the debt within 10 years, but that most of the options would require congressional action. Implementation of the 2014 Act may further reduce the likelihood of repayment within 10 years, because the act reduces future program premium revenue by reinstating subsidized and grandfathered rates the Biggert-Waters Act had eliminated.

As required by the Biggert-Waters Act, FEMA is establishing a reserve fund that could help reduce the need for future borrowing from Treasury, but FEMA will likely not meet the act's annual targets for building up the reserve. The act requires FEMA to create and maintain a reserve fund equal to 1 percent of the total potential loss exposure of all outstanding flood insurance policies in force (reserve ratio) at the end of the prior fiscal year or a higher amount if FEMA chooses.[15] It further requires the reserve to be phased in over time, with at least 7.5 percent of the total added yearly until the reserve is fully funded. The 2014 Act adds an annual surcharge of $25 for residential policies and $250 for nonresidential and nonprimary residential policies.[16] These funds also will be deposited into the reserve fund. In any year that FEMA determines the required reserve ratio cannot be met, FEMA must report to Congress the maximum attainable percentage for the year.[17] As of the end of fiscal year 2013, FEMA had about $1.29 trillion of potential loss exposure, 1 percent of which is $12.9 billion. At the start of

---

[14]Pub. L. No. 112-141, § 100213,126 Stat. 405, 925 (2012). Additionally after borrowing funds, FEMA must report to Congress and the Treasury on the 6-month anniversary and every 6 months thereafter on the progress of the repayment. Id. § 100213(a).

[15]Pub. L. No. 112-141, § 100212, 126 Stat. 405, 992 (2012). The act authorizes the Secretary of the Treasury to invest amounts in the reserve fund in Treasury securities. According to FEMA officials, the interest-earning feature of the reserve fund is one factor to be considered in deciding whether to allocate funds to the reserve, pay down debt, or preserve cash balances. Premiums collected in excess of claims and expenses that are not allocated to the reserve fund do not earn interest.

[16]Pub. L. No. 113-89, § 8.

[17]The report must also (1) describe and detail the specific concerns of the FEMA administrator regarding the consequences of the reserve ratio not being achieved, (2) demonstrate how such consequences would harm the long-term financial soundness of the flood insurance program, and (3) indicate the maximum attainable reserve ratio for that particular fiscal year. Id. § 100212. The 2014 Act requires reporting on a quarterly basis. Pub. L. No. 113-89, § 20.

fiscal year 2014, FEMA began to build the reserve fund by implementing a 5 percent premium surcharge for all policies except those with preferred-risk rates.[18]

On the basis of premiums on policies in force at the end of fiscal year 2013, and not including additional premium surcharges contained in the 2014 Act, FEMA is expected to generate reserve funds in fiscal year 2014 that equal about 20 percent of what the Biggert-Waters Act requires for that year. Using fiscal year 2013's potential loss exposure, table 2 compares the reserving requirements of the Biggert-Waters Act and the 5 percent surcharge that FEMA began implementing in fiscal year 2014. FEMA's ability to raise the required reserve is limited. Specifically, FEMA is not allowed to increase premiums in any single risk class by more that 15 percent in any given year, so it cannot increase premiums by the 25.6 percent that would be necessary to build the reserve fund at the required rate.[19] FEMA officials stated that the 5 percent surcharge was an initial step and that they planned to implement additional increases over the next few years to generate required annual contributions to the reserve fund. FEMA officials said that they plan to report to Congress, as required, on the consequences of the agency's failure to meet the 7.5 percent contribution to the reserve fund in fiscal year 2014.

Table 2: Comparison of NFIP Reserve Fund Requirements to FEMA Actions for Fiscal Year 2014

	Contribution to reserve fund in fiscal year 2014 as a percentage of total mandated reserve amount	Contribution to reserve fund in fiscal year 2014 in dollars	Associated average dollar and percentage premium increase per policy
Biggert-Waters Act requirement	7.5%	$966 million	$174 (25.6%)
FEMA action	1.5% (expected)	$192 million (expected)	$34 (5.0%)

Source: GAO analysis of FEMA data.

Note: FEMA is not allowed to increase premiums in any single risk class by more that 15 percent in any given year, so it cannot increase premiums by the 25.6 percent that would be necessary to build the reserve fund at the required rate. This analysis does not include additional premium surcharges contained in the 2014 Act.

<u>FEMA Could Do More to Ensure Reasonableness of Payments to WYOs</u>

As previously noted, FEMA primarily uses WYO companies to sell and service NFIP policies.[20] From 1969 through 1977, the Department of Housing and Urban Development (HUD), which

---

[18]Properties in moderate-to-low-risk flood zones with minimal flooding history may qualify for lower rates known as preferred-risk rates.

[19]The Biggert-Waters Act imposed a cap on premium increases of 20 percent for each risk class. The 2014 Act reduced the permitted increase to no more than 15 percent for each risk class and no more than 18 percent per property. Pub. L. No. 113-89, § 5.

[20]Private insurers become WYOs by entering into an arrangement with FEMA (the Financial Assistance/Subsidy Arrangement) to issue flood policies in their own name. The insurers must have experience in property and casualty insurance lines, be in good standing with state insurance departments, and be capable of adequately selling and servicing flood insurance policies. They must also comply with the provisions of FEMA's Control Plan, which outlines the companies' responsibilities for program operations, including underwriting, claims adjustments, cash management, and financial reporting, as well as FEMA's responsibilities for management and oversight.

administered NFIP at the time, had an agreement with a consortium of private insurers, known as the National Flood Insurers Association, to sell and service policies. Under this agreement, HUD reimbursed the association for operating costs and provided an annual operating allowance equal to 5 percent of policyholders' premiums. From 1978 to 1983, a federal contractor—not an insurance company—serviced policies, while prospective policyholders continued to go through local agents and brokers to obtain their policies.[21] Because of customer complaints and stagnant policy growth, in 1983, FEMA—which was created and began administering the program in 1979—established the WYO program. As of September 2013, about 85 WYO insurance companies accounted for about 85 percent of the more than 5.5 million flood insurance policies in force. FEMA contracts with a company that serves as the insurer for the remaining 15 percent of policies. Customers with severe repetitive loss properties or group policies must purchase their policies through the FEMA contractor. Additionally, over the past several years, some WYOs have left the program and their policies were transferred to the contractor.

WYOs adjust, settle, and pay flood claims, as well as handle lawsuits arising from claims. Insurance agents from these companies are the main point of contact for most policyholders. Based on information the insurance agents submit, WYOs issue policies, collect premiums, deduct an allowance for commissions and operating expenses from the premiums (15 percent and 13.5 percent, respectively in 2013), and remit the balance to NFIP. In most cases, insurance companies hire subcontractors—flood insurance vendors—to conduct some or all of the day-to-day processing and management of flood insurance policies. When flood losses occur, policyholders report them to their insurance agents, who notify the WYOs. The WYOs review the claims and process approved claims for payment. FEMA reimburses the WYOs from the National Flood Insurance Fund for the amount of the claims plus a percentage of the claims to cover adjusting and processing expenses.[22] Because FEMA's allowances for these claims adjusting and processing expenses are based on claim amounts, in years with higher claims, WYOs receive a larger proportion of total premiums they collect than in years with lower claims. For example, in 2012, a high-claim year due to losses associated with Superstorm Sandy, WYOs received, via deductions from premiums and payments from FEMA, a total of 43.6 percent of total premiums (for commissions, operating expenses, and claims adjusting and processing), compared to 30.4 percent in 2010, a low-claim year.[23] Additionally, WYOs can earn bonuses based on sales criteria established by FEMA.

---

[21]A Chronology of Major Events Affecting the National Flood Insurance Program, The American Institutes for Research, The Pacific Institute for Research and Evaluation, and Deloitte & Touche LLP, prepared for the Federal Emergency Management Agency, October 2002.

[22]FEMA's payments for adjusting claims range from $60 to $1,250 in flat fees for claims up to $50,000. Payments for adjusting claims over $50,000 are based on a percentage of the claim loss, beginning at 3 percent and declining to 2.1 percent for claim losses of more than $250,000. FEMA's payments for processing claims are 1.5 percent of claim losses incurred plus a percentage of premiums.

[23]To calculate these percentages, we used both the portion of the premiums that WYOs deducted as an allowance for commissions and operating expenses and the payments FEMA made to the WYOs as an allowance for claims adjusting and processing expenses. For this report, we used claims that had loss dates in the year examined. In prior work, we used claims made within the year examined, regardless of the loss date. See GAO-07-1078. Additionally, the calculations in our prior work included WYO sales bonuses, while the calculations in this report do not. For these reasons, the percentages presented in this report and in our prior work are not comparable.

However, the reasonableness of FEMA's compensation to WYOs is unclear. As we found in 2009, FEMA does not systematically consider actual flood insurance expense information when it determines the amount it pays WYOs for selling and servicing flood insurance policies and adjusting claims.[24] Rather, since the inception of the WYO program, FEMA has used various proxies for determining the rates at which it pays the WYOs. Consequently, FEMA does not have the information it needs to determine (1) whether its payments are reasonable and (2) the amount of profit to the WYOs that is included in its payments. As part of our 2009 report, we compared expense payments FEMA made to six WYOs to the WYOs' actual expenses for calendar years 2005 through 2007. We found that the payments exceeded actual expenses by $327.1 million, or 16.5 percent of total payments made. We concluded that opportunities existed for FEMA to improve its oversight of the WYO program and ensure that payments to the participating insurance companies were based on actual company expenses, thereby improving the program's cost-effectiveness.

Based on federal internal control standards and federal managerial accounting standards, our 2009 report recommended that FEMA take steps to provide transparency and accountability of its payments to WYOs and to increase the usefulness of the expense data that WYOs report to the National Association of Insurance Commissioners (NAIC).[25,26] These steps included obtaining reasonable assurance that NAIC flood insurance expense data can be considered in setting payment rates that are appropriate and analyzing the amounts of actual expenses and profit in relation to the estimated amounts used in setting payment rates. At that time, FEMA disagreed with these recommendations. However, consistent with our recommendations and a requirement in the Biggert-Waters Act, FEMA officials told us in 2013 that they had made progress in standardizing the reported WYO data and that they would eventually use these data to enhance payment transparency and accountability. The Biggert-Waters Act requires FEMA to finalize a rule with a methodology to pay WYOs based on actual expenses for selling, writing and servicing NFIP policies.[27] The act required FEMA to finalize the rule by July 2013. However, FEMA officials told us they did not expect to complete the development of the methodology to determine reimbursed expenses until sometime in 2014. Additionally, they said the related rulemaking process may take 2 or more additional years.[28]

Our 2009 report also made recommendations designed to improve oversight of the WYO program and compliance with program requirements. More specifically, our recommendations focused on improving the completeness of and compliance with FEMA's Control Plan, which outlines WYO companies' responsibilities for program operations. In addition, citing requirements in the Government Performance and Results Act of 1993, we recommended that

---

[24]GAO, *Opportunities Exist to Improve Oversight of the WYO Program*, GAO-09-455 (Washington, D.C.: Aug. 21, 2009).

[25]GAO, *Standards for Internal Control in the Federal Government*, GAO/AIMD-00-21.3.1 (Washington, D.C.: November 1999).

[26]The National Association of Insurance Commissioners is the U.S. standard-setting and regulatory support organization created and governed by the chief insurance regulators from the 50 states, the District of Columbia, and five U.S. territories.

[27]Pub. L. No. 112-141, § 100224, 126 Stat. 405, 936 (2012).

[28]The act contains a mandate for GAO to report on the efficacy, adequacy, and sufficiency of the final rule no later than 180 days after the final rule's effective date. Pub. L. No. 112-141, § 100224(f), 126 Stat. 405, 937 (2012).

FEMA target its WYO bonus program based on NFIP marketing goals.[29] FEMA implemented these recommendations.

Options Exist to Potentially Reduce NFIP's Costs and Financial Exposure, but They Pose Trade-Offs

As shown in table 3, we have described broad options in previous work that could help reduce NFIP's costs and financial exposure.[30] Each option also poses potential challenges with respect to the impact on the program's public policy goals or implementation complexity. For example, options exist to increase private sector participation in the sale of flood insurance, which could reduce NFIP's financial exposure. These include NFIP providing residual insurance (that is, providing coverage for the highest-risk properties that the private sector is unwilling to insure) and NFIP acting as a reinsurer (that is, charging a premium for assuming the risk of losses above a specified threshold). However, this would represent a significant change from the current system, and the extent to which it would reduce the federal government's risk is uncertain.

---

[29]Pub. L. No. 103-62, 107 Stat. 285 (1993).

[30]See GAO, *Flood Insurance: Options for Addressing the Financial Impact of Subsidized Premium Rates on the National Flood Insurance Program,* GAO-09-20 (Washington, D.C.: Nov. 14, 2008); *Flood Insurance: Public Policy Goals Provide a Framework for Reform,* GAO-11-670T (Washington, D.C.: June 23, 2011); *Flood Insurance: Strategies for Increasing Private Sector Involvement,* GAO-14-127 (Washington, D.C.: Jan. 22, 2014); and GAO-13-607.

Table 3: Options to Potentially Reduce NFIP's Costs and Financial Exposure

Option	Implementation approaches	Potential challenges
Charge full-risk rates for all policies	• Eliminate subsidized and grandfathered rates.	• Reduced affordability of premiums for higher-risk policies.[a] • Participation in NFIP may decline due to higher premiums. • Would require congressional action.
Diversify geographic risk by increasing participation	• Increase the number of properties that are mandated to purchase flood insurance. • Increase outreach and education on NFIP.	• Expanding the mandatory purchase requirement would require congressional action.
Increase mitigation efforts	• Increase appropriations for mitigation programs.	• High per unit cost. • Would require congressional action.
Increase private sector participation in flood insurance[b]	• Secure private reinsurance (as authorized by the Biggert-Waters Act and the 2014 Act).[c] • Alternatively, make NFIP the reinsurer for private insurance. • Make NFIP the residual insurer for only the highest-risk properties. • Require private homeowner insurance to include flood coverage.	• Uncertainty about how much these measures would reduce the government's financial risk. • Significantly changes the current system. • Most implementation approaches would require congressional action.

Source: GAO and Biggert-Waters Act.

[a]The Biggert-Waters Act requires FEMA to study participation and affordability for certain policyholders. Pub.L. No. 112-141, § 100236, 126 Stat. 405, 957 (2012). The study is required to include methods to maintain participation, methods to educate consumers about flood risk, and alternatives to subsidies to address affordability, including means-tested vouchers. FEMA has projected an April 2015 completion date for this study. The 2014 Act provides an additional 18 months—until September 2015—to complete this study. Pub. L. No. 113-89, § 16. It also provides more funding for the study and includes several new requirements, such as identifying options for maintaining affordability if annual premiums increase to an amount greater than 2 percent of the liability coverage on the policy. Further, the 2014 Act requires FEMA to submit to Congress a draft affordability framework, based in part on the affordability study, within 18 months of the study's completion. Pub. L. No. 113-89, § 9.

[b]The Biggert-Waters Act allows the use of private flood insurance to meet the NFIP mandatory coverage requirement for mortgage loans. Pub.L. No. 112-141, § 100239, 126 Stat. 405, 958 (2012).

[c]Pub.L. No. 112-141, § 100232, 126 Stat. 405, 953 (2012); Pub. L. No. 113-89, § 10.

Enclosure II: Premium Rate Setting

Background

FEMA generally bases premium rates for NFIP policies on a property's risk of flooding and several other factors. Specifically, FEMA uses location and property characteristics, such as flood zone designation, elevation of the property relative to the community's base flood elevation (BFE), building type, number of floors, presence of a basement, and the year a structure was built relative to the year of a community's original flood map. Additionally, FEMA uses data on prior claims, coverage amount, and policy deductible amount.

NFIP establishes flood zone designations through its mapping process (see table 4).[31] Areas designated as A, AE, V, or VE zones have a high risk of flooding. FEMA has determined that these areas have a 1 percent or greater annual chance of flooding and refers to them as Special Flood Hazard Areas (SFHA). Areas designated as V or VE zones are located along the coast and have an additional hazard associated with storm waves. Areas with a moderate-to-low risk for flooding are designated as B, C, or X zones. Areas where analysis of the flood risk has not been conducted are designated as D zones.

Table 4: NFIP Flood Zone Designations

Flood zone designation	Risk level
B, C, X	Moderate- to low-risk
A, AE	High-risk
V, VE	High-risk coastal
D	Undetermined risk

Source: FEMA.

As previously noted, FEMA charges full-risk rates for some classes of NFIP policies and subsidized rates for others. FEMA sets full-risk and subsidized rates differently.

---

[31]See enclosure IV for information on FEMA's mapping process.

FEMA's Method for Setting Full-Risk Rates May Not Reflect Actual Flood Risk, Adding to Concerns about NFIP's Financial Stability

According to FEMA, full-risk rates are based on the probability of a given level of flooding, damage estimates based on that level of flooding, and accepted actuarial principles. To determine full-risk rates for properties in Special Flood Hazard Areas (SFHA), FEMA uses a rate model that incorporates data on flood risks generated by a hydrologic model developed and used by the U.S. Army Corps of Engineers (Corps).[32] The rate model combines estimates of the frequency of flooding and magnitude of flood damage. It also factors in certain program costs and costs associated with underinsurance and the deductible amount.[33] For properties in areas that FEMA has designated as having a moderate to low risk of flooding (including properties with preferred-risk policies), rates have been developed based on actuarial and engineering judgments, using the rates generated by the rate model and the historical experience of the high-risk flood zones as benchmarks.[34] According to FEMA officials, FEMA has taken this approach for pricing in these zones because it believes the cost of obtaining the information necessary to develop detailed flood frequency-magnitude relationships for use in the hydrologic model would be extremely high in relation to the benefits.

In 2008, we concluded that FEMA's method for setting full-risk rates may not ensure that the rates accurately reflect the actual risk of flood damage.[35] Specifically, we found that a number of factors may affect the accuracy of the rates FEMA charges, as follows:

- Some data inputs to the rate model were outdated or inaccurate. For example, we found that FEMA relied on flood probabilities from the 1980s and damage estimates that did not fully reflect recent NFIP damage experience.

- FEMA did not require all properties remapped into higher-risk areas to pay rates based on the new designation. We noted that this policy, known as grandfathering, was intended to increase participation in NFIP but had eroded NFIP's ability to charge rates that reflected the risk of flooding. In addition, we noted that FEMA had not tracked the number of grandfathered properties and could not determine their financial impact on the program.

- FEMA used a nationwide rating system combining flood zones across many geographic areas, so individual policies did not always reflect local topographical features that affected their particular flood risk. Some patterns in historical claims and premium data suggested that NFIP's full-risk rates may not always reflect actual flood risk.

---

[32]A hydrologic model is a static or dynamic representation of the process that affects surface water runoff.

[33]Property owners are underinsured when they purchase insurance coverage for less than the value of the property, either by choice or because of limits on the amount of available coverage. A property that is underinsured will tend to have claims that are a greater percentage of the amount of insurance coverage, all other things being equal. To compensate for this tendency, FEMA increases premium rates by an "underinsurance factor" that is based on claims data going back to 1978 for different zones and types of structures. More recent experience is given a greater weight in determining the factors.

[34]The two types of policies in the moderate- to low-risk zones are referred to as preferred risk policies and standard policies. Preferred risk policyholders generally pay the lowest flood rates. Preferred risk policies are available on buildings that are outside of an SFHA and have not flooded more than once.

[35]GAO, *Flood Insurance: FEMA's Rate-Setting Process Warrants Attention*, GAO-09-12 (Washington, D.C.: Oct. 31, 2008).

- Due partly to limitations in its authority, FEMA did not fully take into account ongoing and planned development, long-term trends in erosion, or the effects of global climate change.

As we have found in other prior work, another factor affecting FEMA's full-risk rates is FEMA's lack of authority to increase rates on full-risk policies due to repetitive losses.[36] Repetitive loss structures have historically accounted for a disproportionate share of NFIP insurance claims.[37] The Biggert-Waters Act requires FEMA to increase premiums for subsidized policies with severe repetitive losses to a nonsubsidized amount, but not for full-risk policies with such losses because FEMA cannot charge more than full-risk rates.[38]

Collectively, these factors increase the likelihood that premiums collected on full-risk policies might be insufficient to cover future losses, adding to concerns about NFIP's financial stability. Our 2008 report recommended that FEMA (1) take steps to ensure that its rate-setting methods and the data it uses to set rates result in full-risk premium rates that accurately reflect the risk of losses from flooding and (2) ensure that information is collected on the location, number, and losses associated with existing and newly created grandfathered properties in NFIP and analyze the financial impact of these properties on the flood insurance program. FEMA generally agreed with our recommendations.

FEMA has initiated some actions that are consistent with our recommendations and Biggert-Waters Act provisions that address some of the issues raised in our 2008 report. For example, in December 2013, FEMA officials told us that they had begun collecting information to update flood frequency data used in the rate model and had dedicated funding to the effort for the next 5 to 10 years. Such data could provide FEMA with information on the likely frequency of a Hurricane Katrina-sized storm. The officials also said they were working with Write-Your-Own insurance companies to accurately collect water depth and damage information when adjusting claims to update data on flood damage. Additionally, FEMA began collecting information in 2010 to assess the financial impact of newly grandfathered properties. FEMA had planned to implement a Biggert-Waters Act provision in the second half of 2014 that generally prohibited the grandfathering of rates after future remapping and required any rate increases stemming from future remapping to be phased in over time.[39] However, the 2014 Act generally eliminated the Biggert-Waters Act's changes to grandfathering provisions.[40] Further, under authority provided by the Biggert-Waters Act, FEMA has initiated the process to incorporate long-term erosion and climate change into future mapping efforts.[41] Nevertheless, our 2008

---

[36]For example, see GAO, *Flood Insurance: Options for Addressing the Financial Impact of Subsidized Premium Rates on the National Flood Insurance Program,* GAO-09-20 (Washington, D.C.: Nov. 14, 2008). At the time of this report, FEMA defined a repetitive loss structure as any non-flood-mitigated property with more than one loss over the prior 10 years.

[37]For example, we reported in 2008 that repetitive loss properties accounted for 1 percent of the policies and 30 percent of the claims over the life of the program. See GAO-09-20.

[38]Pub. L. No. 112-141, § 100205, 126 Stat. 405, 917 (2012).

[39]The Biggert-Waters Act did not eliminate grandfathered rates for policies that were currently receiving them. However, prior to passage of the 2014 Act, FEMA's policy was to eliminate grandfathered rates for policies that lapsed as a result of the deliberate choice of the property owner.

[40]Pub. L. No. 113-89, § 4. The 2014 Act included a provision which may prohibit grandfathering in limited situations. Pub. L. No. 113-89, § 6.

[41]Pub. L. No. 112-141, § 100216(b)(3), 126 Stat. 405, 927 (2012).

recommendations remain open because FEMA's actions to address them are in the early stages or do not fully address all of the issues we raised. For instance, FEMA has not collected information on the number and location of existing grandfathered properties, which it needs to assess their financial impact on the program.

The 2014 Act Reinstates Subsidies for Some Policies, but Moving to Full-Risk Rates for Other Policies Poses Challenges

FEMA has taken steps to implement Biggert-Waters Act provisions that require the agency to set premiums that fully reflect the risk of loss from flooding, but implementation of these steps poses challenges.[42] When that legislation was enacted in July 2012, subsidized policies accounted for about 20 percent of all policies, nearly all of which were in SFHAs.[43] FEMA officials told us that, after paying for all administrative and other expenses, subsidized premiums would be sufficient, on average, to pay for less than half of expected claims costs.[44] As FEMA transitions subsidized rates to full-risk rates, policies for properties with a higher risk of flooding could be subject to substantially higher rates. As mandated by the Biggert-Waters Act, FEMA has begun phasing out subsidized premiums on policies for business properties, residential properties that are not primary residences, and single-family (1-4 units) severe repetitive loss properties. In a prior report, we estimated that there were about 438,000 such policies, as of June 2012.[45] FEMA had also begun implementing Biggert-Waters Act provisions to reduce and eventually eliminate most subsidized rates on remaining policies.[46] Our prior report estimated that there were about 715,000 of these policies, as of June 2012. The Biggert-Waters Act, among other restrictions, prohibited subsidies from being passed to new property owners and removed them if insurance coverage lapsed as a result of the policyholders' deliberate choice. However, the 2014 Act permits subsidies for properties that were purchased after July 2012 and properties that initially received insurance after July 2012. It also permits subsidies for certain lapsed policies.[47] The 2014 Act does not reinstate subsidies on policies for nonprimary residences, severe repetitive loss properties, and businesses, among others.

As we found in a July 2013 report, FEMA does not have the information needed to determine the appropriate premium amounts policyholders should pay to reflect the full level of risk for

---

[42]Pub. L. No. 112-141, § 100205, 100207, 126 Stat. 405, 917, 919 (2012).

[43]This percentage does not include grandfathered policies. As previously noted, FEMA does not categorize policies with grandfathered rates as "subsidized" because they are within classes of policies that are not subsidized for the class as a whole, but contain cross-subsidies within the class between nongrandfathered and grandfathered policies.

[44]We plan to conduct additional analysis of the cost of subsidized polices in follow-up work done for *Flood Insurance: More Information Needed on Subsidized Properties*, GAO-13-607 (Washington, D.C.: July 3, 2013).

[45]GAO-13-607.

[46]The Biggert-Waters Act leaves in place discounted rates for properties behind certain unfinished or decertified levees, with some additional procedural requirements, and emergency program properties. Pub. L. No. 112-141, §100230, 126 Stat. 405, 946 (2012).

[47]Pub. L. No. 113-89, § 3. FEMA must refund to certain policyholders premiums paid after July 2012 that exceed the subsidized premiums permissible under the 2014 Act. Purchasers of properties that are covered by a flood insurance policy with subsidized premiums may retain that coverage for the remainder of the term of the policy or until the implementation by FEMA of the 2014 Act.

floods.[48] To phase out and eventually eliminate subsidies remaining after the 2014 Act and to revise rates over time, FEMA will need information on the relative risk of flooding and property elevations, which generally had not been required for subsidized policies prior to the Biggert-Waters Act. Citing federal internal control standards regarding risk analysis, our 2013 report recommended that FEMA develop and implement a plan to obtain flood risk information needed to determine full-risk rates for properties with previously subsidized rates. FEMA agreed with the recommendation and is evaluating the appropriate approach for obtaining or requiring the submittal of this information. In the meantime, the agency plans to assume that holders of all subsidized policies pay about half of the full-risk premium and has begun phasing in rate increases based on this factor for all active policies that are having their subsidies removed.

Premium rate increases arising from the Biggert-Waters Act, such as increases due to the phasing out of some subsidies, could present affordability challenges for some property owners, especially those with low or moderate incomes.[49] For example, FEMA has noted that annual premiums may exceed $10,000 in some high-risk areas. We concluded in January 2014 that higher rates could lead some property owners to purchase lower amounts of coverage or choose not to purchase flood insurance at all.[50] Additionally, higher flood insurance rates could affect property owners' home values and their ability to sell their properties. For example, potential buyers might decide not to purchase a home in a high-risk area after determining the cost of flood insurance for the property. These potential adverse effects have been the subject of congressional hearings and recent legislation.[51] The 2014 Act's repeal of certain rate increases in the Biggert-Waters Act will address affordability concerns for affected property owners. But the repeal may also reduce program revenues and weaken the potential for improved financial soundness of the NFIP program, which would likely prolong the program's long-term burden on taxpayers.

FEMA's Method for Setting Subsidized Rates Evolved Due to Losses from the 2005 Hurricanes

According to FEMA, the process of setting subsidized rates has evolved. In 2008, we reported that to set subsidized rates, FEMA subtracted the amount it expected to collect in full-risk premiums from the average historical loss year—that is, the amount that the program needs to collect from all premiums to cover the average annual losses, as determined by historical data.[52] The difference was the minimum aggregate amount that the program had to collect in subsidized premiums. To set individual subsidized rates, FEMA considered perceived flood risk, previous rate increases for the various flood zones, and statutory limits on rate increases.

---

[48]GAO-13-607.

[49]The Biggert-Waters Act contains a number of other provisions that could lead to higher rates. These include, but are not limited to, provisions that allow FEMA to increase average annual premiums for each risk class more than was previously allowed and require FEMA to build a reserve fund. The 2014 Act caps the amount that average premiums for each risk class can be increased at 15 percent per year.

[50]GAO, *Flood Insurance: Strategies for Increasing Private Sector Involvement,* GAO-14-127 (Washington, D.C.: Jan. 22, 2014).

[51]Homeowner Flood Insurance Affordability Act of 2014, Pub L. No. 113-89 (Mar. 21, 2014).

[52]GAO-09-12.

In February 2014, FEMA officials told us that the process for setting subsidized rates had evolved and involved administrative discretion. The officials said that they revised the definition of average historical loss year and use this benchmark only as a point of comparison. They stated that prior to Hurricane Katrina, the sum of full-risk and subsidized premiums represented about 115 percent of the average historical loss year as originally defined. However, the extreme losses from Hurricane Katrina and other storms in 2005 substantially increased the average historical loss year. FEMA officials told us that if they continued to calculate and use the average historical loss year as they previously had, it would have led to the elimination of subsidized policies. FEMA could not have implemented this policy in the short term because of statutory limits on premium increases. Additionally, FEMA felt that such a major policy change should only be implemented at the direction of Congress. Therefore, in 2007, FEMA chose to base subsidized rate increases on a revised calculation of the average historical loss year, which gives partial weight to the 2005 losses.[53] The 2005 losses significantly increased the average historical loss year, leading to sizeable increases in subsidized premiums in 2008 and 2009.[54] According to FEMA, between 2007 and 2012, the agency collected total premiums above the revised calculation of the average historical loss year. As part of future work on NFIP, we plan to examine FEMA's rate-setting process and how it has changed in response to the Biggert-Waters Act and the 2014 Act.

---

[53]FEMA's method gives a 1 percent weight to the 2005 losses. FEMA officials said this practice was consistent with the Biggert-Waters Act requirement that the calculation of an average historical loss year include catastrophic loss years, because the act does not prescribe the exact formula for including catastrophic loss years. Additionally, the officials said that the method for including catastrophic loss years should ideally be one that continues to work effectively over a wide range of possible future scenarios. They said that partly for this reason, FEMA actuaries chose not to give full weight to the 2005 experience.

[54]The average historical loss year would have been even bigger if the 2005 losses had been given full weight rather than partial weight.

Enclosure III: Community and Property Owner Participation

Background

Both communities and property owners participate in NFIP.[55] Community participation is voluntary but is particularly important because property owners can purchase NFIP policies only if their communities join the program. Participating communities agree to take steps to mitigate flood risk by enforcing building codes and managing floodplains. The proportion of all properties with flood insurance is known as the flood insurance penetration rate.

Any property owner in a participating community may purchase flood insurance. However, certain property owners in special flood hazard areas (SFHA)—areas at high risk for flooding—are subject to the mandatory purchase requirement and must retain flood insurance for the life of their mortgage loans.[56] They include, but are not limited to property owners in participating communities: (1) who obtain loans from lending institutions generally regulated by the Board of Governors of the Federal Reserve System, the Farm Credit Administration, the Federal Deposit Insurance Corporation, the National Credit Union Administration, and the Office of the Comptroller of the Currency; (2) whose loans have been purchased by Fannie Mae or Freddie Mac; and (3) whose loans are insured or guaranteed by a federal agency such as the Federal Housing Administration or the Veterans Administration.

Flood Insurance Penetration Rates Are Estimated to be Low, and Information on Compliance with Mandatory Purchase Requirement Is Limited

As we have previously found, nationwide NFIP penetration rates for single-family homes are estimated to be low based on limited data.[57] These estimates illustrate the potential to increase the number of property owners with flood insurance coverage. For example, based on data from a sample of single-family homes in 100 communities, a 2006 RAND study estimated that, on average, the penetration rate in SFHAs nationwide was about 50 percent, even though many property owners in SFHAs were required to purchase flood insurance.[58] As of September 2013, about 61 percent of NFIP policies were in SFHAs. The study also found variations in penetration rates in SFHAs across regions and communities.[59] The same study estimated that, on average, the penetration rate for single-family homes in non-SFHAs was about 1 percent.

---

[55]FEMA defines an NFIP community as any state, any area or political subdivision of a state, or any Indian tribe or authorized tribal organization, that has the authority to adopt and enforce floodplain management regulations for its jurisdiction. See 44 C.F.R. § 59.1.

[56]44 C.F.R. § 64.3(b); 42 U.S.C. § 4012a(a).

[57]GAO, *Flood Insurance: Options for Addressing the Financial Impact of Subsidized Premium Rates on the National Flood Insurance Program,* GAO-09-20 (Washington, D.C.: Nov. 14, 2008).

[58]RAND, *The National Flood Insurance Program's Market Penetration Rate: Estimates and Policy Implications* (Santa Monica, Calif.: 2006).

[59]For example, in the South and the West, the study estimated penetration rates of about 60 percent, but estimated penetration rates of about 20 to 30 percent in the Northeast and Midwest.

However, the RAND study also discussed several limitations in the data and methodology used. For example, the authors noted that their sample sizes for some regions were either "modest" or were estimated with a considerable degree of uncertainty. Further, because the total number of properties in a flood zone might be unknown, determining the proportion of property owners with flood insurance was difficult. As a result of these limitations, the authors said the study's nationwide estimate of the number of single-family homes in SFHAs may be 10 to 15 percent lower than the actual rate. The RAND study also cited other data limitations that we had encountered when attempting to make similar estimates, such as matching addresses in NFIP and real estate data.[60] Owing to a lack of relevant real estate data, the study excluded about two-thirds of NFIP communities from the universe of NFIP communities from which the study sample was drawn. For all of these reasons, the estimated penetration rates lack precision.

According to FEMA officials, FEMA has contracted with a vendor to conduct a new penetration rate study using geospatial information system (GIS) technology. The vendor is comparing commercially available geospatial coordinates of residential properties with SFHAs on FEMA's flood maps. In December 2013, FEMA officials stated that the agency was evaluating the contractor's initial analysis and assessing its reliability.

As we have previously found, information on the extent of compliance with the mandatory purchase requirement is limited.[61] Mortgage lenders and servicers are responsible for verifying that property owners have purchased flood insurance and were maintaining it for properties in SFHAs. The 2006 RAND study previously discussed estimated that nationwide compliance with purchase requirements, under plausible assumptions, appeared to be 75 to 80 percent in SFHAs for single-family homes.[62] However, as discussed above, the authors of this study faced data limitations. The authors noted that it was not possible to make precise estimates of the percentage of homes complying with the mandatory purchase requirement based on the data assembled for the study because the data did not reliably show whether a home had a mortgage or whether the mortgage was subject to the mandatory purchase requirement. Another research organization found that homeowners both within and outside SFHAs did not maintain flood policies.[63] Specifically, it showed that policies were held for a median of 2 to 4 years. However, on the basis of our analysis of the annual rate at which the number of subsidized policies had declined, we determined that the 2- to 4-year average was an underestimate.[64] According to FEMA officials, the vendor performing the penetration rate study

---

[60] GAO-09-20.

[61] GAO, *Federal Emergency Management Agency: Ongoing Challenges Facing the National Flood Insurance Program,* GAO-08-118T (Washington, D.C.: Oct. 2, 2007).

[62] Assumptions made in calculating compliance rates were as follows: (1) the number of policies underwritten by private insurers is 7 percent of the number of NFIP policies in SFHAs; (2) 85 percent of mortgages in SFHAs are subject to the mandatory purchase requirement; and (3) the market penetration rates for homes that have mortgages but are not subject to the mandatory purchase requirement is 38 percent.

[63] Erwann Michel-Kerjan, Sabine Lemoyne de Forges, and Howard Kunreuther, "Policy Tenure Under the U.S. National Flood Insurance Program (NFIP)," *Risk Analysis,* vol. 32, no. 4 (April 2012).

[64] GAO, *Flood Insurance: More Information Needed on Subsidized Properties,* GAO-13-607 (Washington, D.C.: July 3, 2013). We compared our results to the research organization's results by calculating the average decline rate from their published tenure duration results. Our analysis showed about a 5 percent slower decline rate than this study. The difference was due in part to the data differences. We were able to determine when policyholders changed insurance carriers whereas these data were not available for the research organization.

will also match GIS and flood policy data to mortgage data to assess compliance with the mandatory purchase requirement.

The Biggert-Waters Act increased the penalties on lenders for not enforcing the mandatory purchase requirements and on the GSEs for purchasing loans without proper flood insurance from $350 to $2,000 per violation and eliminated the institutional cap on penalties.[65] As required by the 1994 amendments to the National Flood Insurance Act, the regulatory agencies established rules directing lending institutions not to make loans secured by improved real estate located in SFHAs unless flood insurance had been purchased.

Although Many Property Owners Participate in NFIP, Several Factors Limit Participation

As of September 30, 2013, there were more than 5.5 million NFIP policies in force in the approximately 22,000 communities participating in the program.[66] As shown in figure 1, participation increased markedly after the National Flood Insurance Reform Act of 1994—which expanded the mandatory purchase requirement for federally backed mortgages on properties located in SFHAs—and after the major hurricanes in 2004 and 2005.[67] The number of policies rose from 3.0 million to 4.1 million from 1994 through 1997 and from 4.7 million to 5.5 million from 2004 through 2006. The number of policies in New York and New Jersey increased substantially after Superstorm Sandy in 2012, but the nationwide number of policies remained about the same.

Figure 1: Number of NFIP Policies in Force, 1978-2013

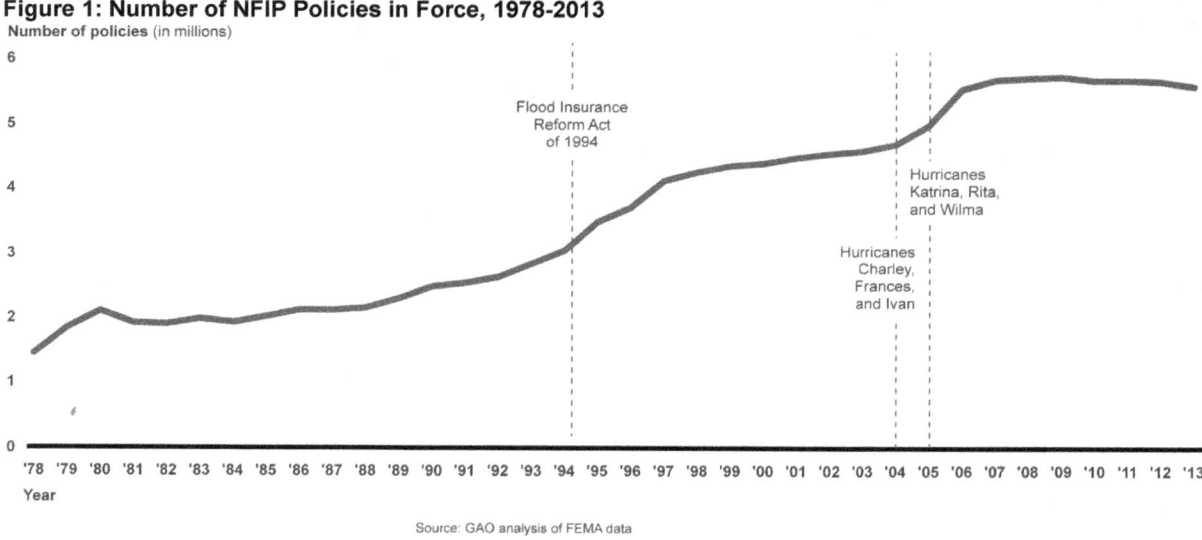

Source: GAO analysis of FEMA data

---

[65]Pub. L. No. 112-141, §100208, 126 Stat. 405, 919 (2012).

[66]This number represented more than 90 percent of the communities identified by FEMA as having some degree of flood risk. Some communities may face barriers to participation. For example, we reported in 2013 that some Native American tribes lacked jurisdiction to adopt and enforce the land use ordinances that were required for NFIP participation. Instead, many have lands that were allotted to individuals rather than to a tribal entity, limiting the tribes' jurisdiction. See GAO, *Flood Insurance: Participation of Indian Tribes in Federal and Private Programs*, GAO-13-226 (Washington, D.C.: Jan. 4, 2013).

[67]National Flood Insurance Reform Act of 1994, § 522, 108 Stat. 2160, 2257 (1994).

Despite these increases, NFIP stakeholders have cited several factors that limit property owner's participation in NFIP, as we reported in January 2014.[68]

- First, many property owners have an inaccurate perception of their risk of flooding. For example, some property owners outside of SFHAs believe that only properties in SFHAs are at risk. Additionally, some property owners inside SFHAs believe they are not at risk because a flood will happen only once every 100 years. FEMA's previous designation of SFHAs as lying within a "100-year" flood zone contributed to this misperception. However, FEMA replaced this terminology by describing SFHAs as areas with "a 1-percent annual chance of flooding." The Biggert-Waters Act amended the Real Estate Settlement Procedures Act to require that homebuyers be provided an explanation of flood insurance regardless of a property's flood zone designation.[69] Additionally, the 2014 Act requires FEMA to clearly communicate full flood risk determinations to individual property owners, regardless of whether their premium rates are full actuarial rates.[70]

- Second, some property owners inaccurately assume that flood perils are included in their homeowners insurance policies or that they will receive federal or state disaster assistance in response to a flood event. Flooding is generally excluded from homeowners' insurance policies, however, and property owners are eligible for federal relief only under certain circumstances and up to certain limits.

- Third, one lending institution told us that they did not perceive flood risk to threaten their safety and soundness and therefore often did not require flood insurance coverage at mortgage origination unless it was specifically required by federal law.

- Finally, flood insurance can be quite expensive, especially for nonsubsidized properties that lie within SFHAs and are below the Base Flood Elevation (BFE).[71] For example, annual premiums for such properties can exceed $10,000. As discussed in enclosure II, properties with insurance subsidies pay only a portion of the actual cost of their flood insurance premium, and properties that do not have subsidies reinstated by the 2014 Act may experience a significant jump in premium costs. We reported in 2013 on two related options that could allow certain groups to purchase flood insurance at a potentially lower cost than under NFIP.[72] The first would involve expanding the existing eligible flood insurance risk-sharing pools to obtain the critical mass of policies necessary to make low-cost flood insurance policies affordable. The second would establish a new private "microinsurance"

---

[68]GAO, *Flood Insurance: Strategies for Increasing Private Sector Involvement,* GAO-14-127 (Washington, D.C.: Jan. 22, 2014).

[69]Pub. L. No. 112-141, §100222, 126 Stat. 405, 934 (2012) and Real Estate Settlement Procedures Act (RESPA), 12 U.S.C. § 2601, et seq. The 2014 Act amended RESPA to require that property owners be notified that they are responsible for all flood damage if they choose to forego coverage on detached structures. Pub. L. No. 113-89, § 13.

[70]Pub. L. No. 113-89, § 28.

[71]BFE is the computed elevation to which floodwater is anticipated to rise during a flood that is estimated to have a 1 percent chance of occurring annually.

[72]GAO-13-226. Although this report focuses on Indian tribes, the options we discuss potentially have broader applicability.

program offering low-premium policies with small coverage limits based on similar operations in developing countries. FEMA said that its NFIP privatization study mandated by the Biggert-Waters Act would include an assessment of these alternatives. In addition, the 2014 Act requires FEMA to study options for making available voluntary community-based flood insurance policies.[73]

The Biggert-Waters Act and the 2014 Act also contain provisions that address certain challenges to property owner participation. For example, the Biggert-Waters Act required federally regulated lending institutions to escrow insurance premiums and fees for flood insurance on residential improved real estate unless the regulated lending institution meets a small institution exception.[74] The 2014 Act effectively delayed implementation until January 2016 and added exclusions to the escrow requirement.[75] Following the Biggert-Waters Act, property owners no longer had to pay an entire annual premium in a single payment. The 2014 Act clarified this change by permitting FEMA to provide property owners who do not have their fees collected through escrow with the option of paying premiums annually or in monthly installments.[76] Finally, the Biggert-Waters Act also required that NFIP policies state the conditions, exclusions, and limits to coverage in plain English and in large boldface type.[77]

FEMA Has Taken Steps to Increase Penetration Rates and Outreach for NFIP

One of the public policy goals we used in a January 2014 report for evaluating options for increasing private sector involvement in flood insurance was encouraging property owners to purchase flood insurance coverage.[78] FEMA is responsible for marketing NFIP and reaching out to property owners and stakeholders and has made outreach efforts to communities and homeowners. For example, FEMA offers emergency management training for community officials and a website, *floodsmart.gov*, for property owners that contains information about flood risk and insurance rates and tools to determine flood risk and find an insurance agent. Additionally, FEMA has modified the sales bonuses it provides to Write-Your-Own insurance companies to align with low participation areas.[79]

FEMA also has specific outreach requirements for communicating to communities about new and updated maps. Federal regulations require FEMA to communicate potential changes in flood risk to community stakeholders when it decides to initiate a flood mapping study. When it

---

[73]Pub. L. No. 113-89, § 23. Further, the 2014 Act contains a mandate for GAO to report any comments on FEMA's report no later than 6 months after FEMA submits it to Congress Pub. L. No. 113-89, § 23.

[74]Pub. L. No. 112-141, §100209, 126 Stat. 405, 920 (2012); Pub. L. No. 112-281, 126 Stat. 2485 (2013).

[75]The exclusions include, among other things, subordinate lien loans and home equity lines of credit. Pub. L. No. 113-89, §25.

[76]Pub. L. No. 112-141, §100205, 126 Stat. 405, 917 (2012); Pub. L. No. 113-89, § 11.

[77]Pub. L. No. 112-141, §100234, 126 Stat. 405, 956 (2012).

[78]GAO-14-127.

[79]FEMA sells and services NFIP policies primarily through private insurance companies that participate in the Write-Your-Own program.

is ready to release preliminary maps, FEMA must publish the proposed base flood elevations in the *Federal Register* for public comment and in a prominent local newspaper in the community, and notify the community of the results of the study. When the final map is approved and implemented, FEMA must publish another *Federal Register* notice. The 2014 Act requires, before commencement of any mapping or map updating process, that FEMA notify each community affected of the model or models that FEMA plans to use and provide an explanation of why such model or models are appropriate.[80]

We found in 2010 that FEMA had taken a variety of steps to conduct outreach to state and local officials, including developing a national outreach strategy.[81] Based on federal internal control standards and requirements in the Government Performance and Results Act of 1993, we recommended that FEMA take a number of steps to enhance its efforts to improve public awareness and promote map acceptance.[82] For example, we recommended that FEMA develop performance goals or measures that could help in determining whether its outreach efforts were achieving their intended results. In addition, we recommended that FEMA identify, allocate, and leverage the resources needed to support national outreach efforts. FEMA has implemented these recommendations. Additionally, FEMA annually surveys the general public and local officials about flood risk and working cooperatively with other agencies to increase flood awareness and encourage mitigation. The 2014 Act requires FEMA to designate a Flood Insurance Advocate, whose duties include educating property owners and policyholders about NFIP and coordinating outreach and education with local officials regarding flood map changes.[83]

---

[80]Pub. L. No. 113-89, § 30. The 2014 Act also requires that FEMA provide each community affected a 30-day period beginning upon notification to consult with FEMA regarding the appropriateness of the mapping model or models to be used.

[81]GAO, *FEMA Flood Maps: Some Standards and Processes in Place to Promote Map Accuracy and Outreach, but Opportunities Exist to Address Implementation Challenges,* GAO-11-17 (Washington, D.C.: Dec. 2, 2010).

[82]Specifically, controls should generally be designed to ensure that ongoing monitoring occurs in the course of normal operations, and agencies should establish policies and procedures, techniques, and mechanisms to enforce management's directives.

[83]Pub. L. No. 113-89, § 24.

Enclosure IV: Flood Mapping

Background

Flood maps, known as flood insurance rate maps (FIRM), serve several purposes. Flood maps provide the basis for setting insurance rates and identifying properties whose owners are required to purchase flood insurance. Flood maps also provide the basis for establishing floodplain building standards that communities must adopt and enforce as part of their NFIP participation. Flood maps include statistical information such as data for river flow, storm tides, hydrologic/hydraulic analyses, and rainfall and topographic surveys. FEMA's Federal Insurance and Mitigation Administration, which manages NFIP, includes a Risk Analysis Division that is responsible for flood mapping activities and developing flood mapping policy and guidance.

A Variety of Stakeholders Help Develop Flood Maps

Stakeholders from all levels of government and the private sector participate in the mapping process. As we described in a December 2010 report, FEMA identifies flood hazards, assesses flood risks, and provides appropriate flood hazard and risk information to communities nationwide.[84] Staff from FEMA's 10 regional offices oversee meetings between all mapping partners, manage the mapping process, and attend public meetings, among other things.

As we concluded in our 2004 report, the ultimate success of FEMA's flood mapping program depends on the level of community investment and involvement in the process.[85] FEMA relies on local governments to provide it with notification of changes in communities that can pose new flood hazards and works with localities to collect the information needed to update flood maps. Changes to communities, such as new development, can affect floodplain boundaries, as shown in figure 2.

---

[84]GAO, *FEMA Flood Maps: Some Standards and Processes in Place to Promote Map Accuracy and Outreach, but Opportunities Exist to Address Implementation Challenges,* GAO-11-17 (Washington, D.C.: Dec. 2, 2010).

[85]GAO, *Flood Map Modernization: Program Strategy Shows Promise, but Challenges Remain,* GAO-04-417 (Washington, D.C.: Mar. 31, 2004).

Figure 2: Effects of Development on a Riverine Floodplain

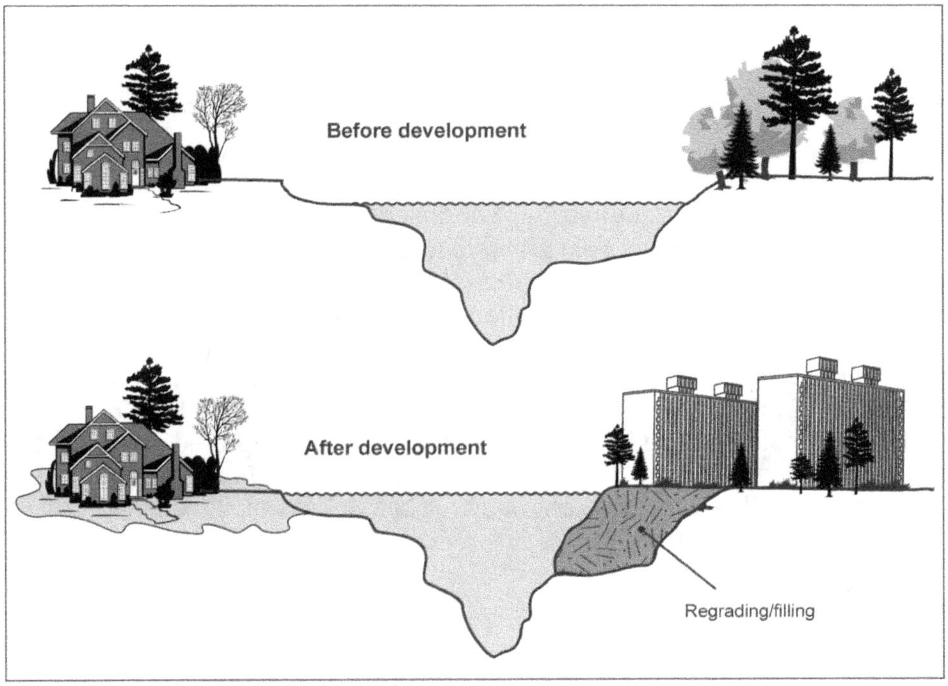

Sources: GAO analysis of FEMA data; Art Explosion (images).

FEMA also relies on mapping partners from the private sector and other federal agencies.[86] Contractors, technical partners, and other federal agencies assist in meetings to discuss the project area that a new mapping project will be starting, collect required data or validate existing data, help FEMA administer mapping activities, create preliminary and final maps, and resolve appeals, among other things. Community members attend public meetings, provide feedback on preliminary maps, and may file appeals to preliminary maps.[87] As previously noted, the 2014 Act requires, before commencement of any mapping or map updating process, that FEMA notify each community affected of the model or models that FEMA plans to use and provide an explanation of why such model or models are appropriate.[88] Additionally, the responsibilities of the FEMA Flood Insurance Advocate created by the 2014 Act include advocating for the fair

---

[86]Other federal agencies that work under interagency agreements with FEMA could include, for example, the U.S. Army Corps of Engineers, Natural Resources Conservation Service, U.S. Geological Survey, National Oceanic and Atmospheric Administration, and Tennessee Valley Authority.

[87]Anyone who owns or leases real property in the affected area who believes that FEMA's proposed base flood elevations or Special Flood Hazard Area delineations would adversely affect his or her property rights may appeal to the local government. The proposed changes must be published twice in the local newspaper, and an appeal must be filed within 90 days of the second notice. Appeals must be based on scientific or technical information showing that the proposed changes are incorrect. Private persons may also initiate appeals that may be heard by FEMA through the community where the property is located. See 42 U.S.C. § 4104.

[88]Pub. L. No. 113-89, § 30. The 2014 Act also requires that FEMA provide each community affected a 30-day period beginning upon notification to consult with FEMA regarding the appropriateness of the mapping model or models to be used.

treatment of policyholders and property owners in the mapping of flood hazards, the identification of risks from flood, and the implementation of measures to minimize the risk of flood.[89]

The Flood Mapping Process and Map Modernization

Flood mapping is a complex and technical endeavor, as we described in a 2011 report.[90] In order to create a map, engineers must conduct field surveys to assess the area to be studied and then develop topographic data on the elevation of the terrain. Engineers also estimate the risk of flooding by analyzing the hydrologic conditions affecting the amount of water that flows downstream during a flood. For example, soil and vegetation absorb rain and reduce runoff, while pavement and other impermeable manmade surfaces increase the flow of runoff and thus the risk of flooding. The results of the topographic and flood hazard analyses are then combined and integrated into digital maps that describe floodplain boundaries and the projected height of the flood waters (base flood elevation). Figure 3 illustrates the boundary and base flood elevation for a riverine floodplain. FEMA also creates maps for coastal areas, which involves consideration of wave height and storm surge.

Figure 3: Riverine Floodplain Boundary and the Base Flood Elevation

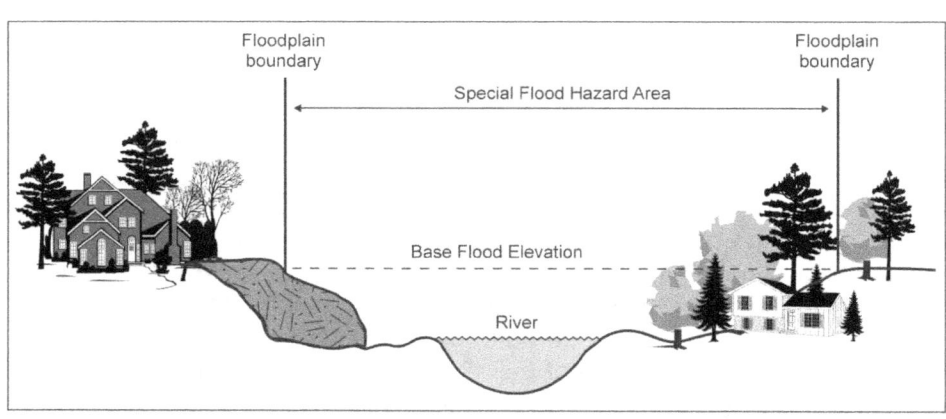

Sources: GAO analysis of FEMA data; Art Explosion (images).

Notes: A Special Flood Hazard Area has an estimated 1 percent annual chance of flooding. The base flood elevation is the height of a flood that has a 1 percent chance of being equaled or exceeded in a given year.

Even when floodplains are mapped with a high level of accuracy, however, land development and natural changes to the landscape and hydrologic systems mean that the maps need to be updated regularly. The National Flood Insurance Reform Act of 1994 requires that, at least every 5 years, FEMA assess the need to revise and update all floodplain areas and flood risk zones, and established the Technical Mapping Advisory Council (TMAC) to provide FEMA with

---

[89]Pub. L. No. 113-89, § 24.

[90]GAO-11-17.

expert input on mapping issues.[91] TMAC (which existed from November 1995 through November 2000) and FEMA also worked collaboratively to shape a program for modernizing maps. As a result of these efforts, in 1997 FEMA developed its initial Map Modernization Plan, which outlined the steps necessary to update the nation's flood maps from paper to digital format. From fiscal years 2003 through 2008, FEMA spent $1.2 billion for its Flood Map Modernization Program (Map Modernization) to create digital flood maps. Through this program, FEMA created digital flood maps for more than 92 percent of the population.[92] FEMA initiated the final year of production under Map Modernization in 2008. In fiscal year 2009, FEMA began a 5-year effort— Risk Mapping, Assessment, and Planning (Risk MAP)—to build on the flood hazard data and maps produced during the Map Modernization program. FEMA also began reviewing 20 percent of the nation's flood maps annually. Risk MAP integrates NFIP flood hazard data with risk assessments that serve as the basis for local hazard mitigation plans and support community actions to reduce risk. Risk MAP received $325 million in appropriations in fiscal year 2009, but appropriations have declined since, falling to about $208 million in fiscal year 2013.

The Biggert-Waters Act required FEMA to reestablish TMAC to deal with map modernization issues. The act requires this council to produce a report for FEMA on the risk assessment and modeling of future conditions by July 6, 2013. The report was to include recommendations on how to ensure that FIRMs incorporated the best available climate science and that FEMA used the best available methodology to consider the impact of rising sea levels and future development on flood risk. FEMA is required to incorporate the council's report into its ongoing program to review and update rate maps. According to FEMA officials, DHS approved a charter for the council in August 2013. In November 2013, FEMA published a notice in the *Federal Register* requesting applications through December 2013 from qualified individuals wishing to be appointed to the council.

The Biggert-Waters Act also stated that FIRMs should reflect:

- all populated areas and areas of possible population growth located within floodplains that have either a 1 percent or 0.2 percent annual chance of flooding;

- areas protected by levees, dams, and other flood control devices;

- areas that could be inundated as a result of the failure of a levee, dam, or other flood control structure; and

---

[91]Pub. L. No. 103-325, §575, 576, 108 Stat. 2255, 2278, 2280 (1994). TMAC was comprised of representatives from federal and state government agencies and professional organizations, based on their demonstrated knowledge and competence regarding surveying, cartography, remote sensing, geographic information systems, or the technical aspects of preparing and using flood maps.

[92]The process of digitizing maps did not necessarily involve reassessment of flood risk.

- the level of protection provided by flood control structures.[93]

In addition, the act states that mapping-related appeals by private persons must be limited to issues of scientific or technical correctness and requires FEMA to have the National Academy of Public Administration study how FEMA can improve interagency coordination related to mapping.[94] The academy issued this report in November 2013.[95]

FEMA Has Addressed Some Levee-Related Concerns and Must Address New Requirements

Levees and floodwalls are typically built parallel to a waterway, most often a river, in order to reduce the risk of flooding to the area behind the structure. Floodwalls, which are typically made of concrete or steel, are often constructed on a levee crown to increase the height of the levee without increasing the base of the embankment.

FEMA is responsible for issuing levee accreditations for the purposes of NFIP. Under NFIP regulations, FEMA generally requires levee owners or community officials seeking to demonstrate that the flood protection provided by a levee submit an engineering certification indicating that the levee complies with certain criteria.[96] If FEMA provides accreditation for the levee, homeowners who reside in the protected area are not subject to the federal requirement to purchase flood insurance, although they have the option to buy flood insurance if they choose.

The U.S. Army Corps of Engineers (Corps) participates in flood damage reduction projects such as levees and floodwalls, and shares the cost of these projects with the project sponsors. In certain limited situations, the Corps may provide the engineering data that the levee owners submit to FEMA for accreditation purposes. However, in most cases local sponsors are responsible for operating and maintaining levees, and federal assistance to locally operated levees is limited by factors such as the availability of federal funding.

As we described in a 2011 report, FEMA's Map Modernization program required communities and levee owners to validate that their levees met FEMA's accreditation requirements.[97] Levee owners said at the time that it was difficult to obtain and pay for accreditation or reaccreditation, and communities expressed concerns about the accreditation process. In July 2010, the

---

[93]The Biggert-Waters Act also detailed specific scientific consideration that should be included when updating maps, including any relevant information on coastal inundation from U.S. Army Corps of Engineers maps and National Oceanic and Atmospheric Administration (NOAA) storm surge modeling; relevant U.S. Geological Survey (USGS) information including on stream flows, watershed characteristics and topography; relevant information on land subsidence, coastal erosion areas, changing lake levels and other flood-related hazards; relevant information from NOAA and USGS relating to best available science regarding future changes in sea level, precipitation, and hurricane intensity; and other relevant information as recommended by TMAC. Pub. L. No. 112-141, §100216(b)(3), 126 Stat. 405, 928 (2012).

[94]Pub. L. No. 112-141, §100217, 100221, 126 Stat. 405, 930, 933-934 (2012).

[95]National Academy of Public Administration, *FEMA Flood Mapping: Enhancing Coordination to Maximize Performance* (Washington, D.C.: Nov. 8, 2013).

[96]44 C.F.R. § 65.10(e).

[97]GAO, *FEMA and the Corps Have Taken Steps to Establish a Task Force, but FEMA Has Not Assessed the Costs of Collecting and Reporting All Levee-Related Concerns,* GAO-11-689R (Washington, D.C.: July 29, 2011).

President signed the Supplemental Appropriations Act, 2010.[98] Language in the Senate committee report accompanying the appropriations act directed FEMA to establish an interagency task force with the Corps and the Office of Management and Budget to track, address, and, where possible, resolve concerns stemming from FEMA's mapping efforts in communities with issues related to flood control infrastructure, including levees. The report also directed the task force to report quarterly to Congress with a list of contacts made by a community official to FEMA or the Corps, including the date of each contact, a brief summary of the concern, and the joint response. Our 2011 report discussed FEMA's view that developing such a tracking system would be unduly resource intensive but also stated that FEMA had not analyzed the costs of developing the system. Federal internal control standards highlight the importance of capturing the information needed to meet program objectives and ensuring that relevant, reliable, and timely information was available to help management make decisions.[99] Therefore, we recommended that FEMA assess the costs of and time frames required to develop a system to collect and report all contact with communities that had levee-related concerns; identify, if applicable, cost-effective alternatives for addressing the reporting requirement; and communicate this information to Congress. In response to our recommendations, FEMA estimated that it would cost from $4 million to $6 million to build, implement, and maintain such a system.[100]

The Biggert-Waters Act also required FEMA to contract with the National Academy of Sciences to study risk models, flood zones, and insurance rates for areas behind levees. In March 2013 the academy issued a report on levees and NFIP, and in July 2013 FEMA issued a report that described a new process for analyzing and mapping areas on the landward side of nonaccredited levee systems that were shown on flood maps.[101] FEMA officials told us that pilot projects were under way in 25 locations using the new levee analysis and mapping process and that the agency intended to implement pilot projects in 30 more locations in fiscal year 2014. The officials stated that following the pilots, they will implement the process in up to 250 more locations nationwide, subject to funding availability.

FEMA Has Taken Steps to Address Challenges in Map Accuracy and Must Incorporate Expert Recommendations

Ensuring the accuracy of flood maps has been a challenge for FEMA, as evidenced by prior assessments of FEMA's mapping efforts. Without accurate and updated flood hazard maps, property owners and small businesses could underestimate their exposure to flood risks and make poor financial decisions about protecting their properties (that is, where to build and whether to purchase flood insurance or take other measures to protect their properties).

---

[98]Pub. L. No. 111-212, 124 Stat. 2302 (2010).

[99]GAO/AIMD-00-21.3.1.

[100]FEMA officials noted that this estimate is only for a system to be built and managed for FEMA use, and did not include costs to build a system for Corps activities.

[101]National Research Council, *Levees and the National Flood Insurance Program: Improving Policies and Practices* (Washington, D.C.: Mar. 2013) and FEMA, *Analysis and Mapping Procedures for Non-Accredited Levee Systems: New Approach* (July 2013).

In our 2004 report on FEMA's mapping program, we assessed FEMA's plans to develop digital flood maps that incorporated specific and accurate data commensurate with communities' relative flood risk.[102] We found that FEMA had not yet established data standards that described the appropriate level of detail, accuracy, and analysis required to develop digital maps based on risk level. Defining the level of data collection and analysis for different levels of risk is important because obtaining and analyzing flood map data are time-consuming and expensive; the more detailed and specific the data, generally the greater the effort and costs to obtain it. We also reviewed FEMA's partnerships with states and local entities that conducted mapping activities and found that FEMA had not yet developed a clear strategy for partnering with communities with few resources and little or no experience in flood mapping. Building and maintaining mutually beneficial partnerships, a FEMA objective, is designed to facilitate and support the efficient production and effective use of flood maps. To help ensure that FEMA's mapping effort produced more accurate flood maps, we made several recommendations. For example, we recommended that FEMA develop and implement data standards for mapping floods as well as strategies for partnering with state and local entities whose capabilities vary. In response to our recommendations, FEMA published plans for strengthening its mapping and floodplain management efforts. The plan addresses the variations in resources and technical expertise among government entities.

Our 2010 report on FEMA's flood mapping efforts found that the agency had taken steps to increase map accuracy.[103] For example, we found that FEMA had developed three standards and a quality assurance process to track compliance with them. These standards are:

- *Guidelines and Specifications for Flood Hazard Mapping Partners.* FEMA published this guide in February 2002 to define technical requirements, product specifications for flood maps and related NFIP products, and associated coordination and documentation activities. FEMA has updated components of the guidelines over time.

- *Floodplain Boundary Standard (FBS).* In response to stakeholder concerns about the quality of flood data used to develop new flood maps during the Map Modernization program, FEMA issued the FBS in October 2007. The FBS was intended, in part, to help ensure that flood maps were tied to a topographic source—that is, that the floodplain boundary and base flood elevation lines drawn on flood maps are comparable to the topographic data selected for the study area. Since 2006, FEMA has required that all flood map studies comply with the FBS.

- *New, Validated, or Updated Engineering (NVUE) Standard.* FEMA also developed the NVUE standard to provide a basis for assessing the engineering analysis used to develop flood elevations. The standard is intended to help mapping partners determine where new study data should be collected, where updates to existing flood hazard data should be performed, and whether previously developed flood study data could still be considered valid. FEMA issued draft guidance for validating existing data in April 2007.

---

[102]*GAO, Flood Map Modernization: Program Strategy Shows Promise, but Challenges Remain,* GAO-04-417 (Washington, D.C.: Mar. 31, 2004).

[103]GAO-11-17.

FEMA established a quality assurance management system under both its Map Modernization program and Risk MAP to help ensure that mapping products and processes comply with FEMA's specified requirements. The quality assurance system includes independent contracted audits of the mapping process that include information not only on compliance but also on the audit methodology.

Our 2010 report also found that FEMA had enhanced its guidance for topographic data by establishing risk-based standards. Specifically, in September 2010 FEMA published Procedural Memorandum 61, which updated its *Guidelines and Specifications* to require mapping partners to align FEMA's topographic data specifications with levels of flood risk and to account for differing characteristics of elevation that can affect the accuracy and precision of base flood elevations. The memorandum identifies the specifications of elevation accuracy and precision needed based on FEMA's risk classes for all 3,146 U.S. counties. Also, prior to issuing the updated guidance, FEMA delineated floodplains using the "best available" existing topographic data, which was sometimes over 35 years old.

At the time of our 2010 review, FEMA planned to work with local officials to determine whether the existing data held by the locality or another source (such as the U.S. Geological Survey) met the new topographic standards or whether to develop new data through means such as Light Detection and Ranging (LIDAR). FEMA has promoted the use of LIDAR remote sensing technologies to generate highly accurate, digital elevation data. As shown in figure 4, an airplane equipped with laser-pulsing sensors using LIDAR measure the contours and crevices that determine where floodwaters collect to provide digital elevation data, which are key to determining flood risk and identifying floodplain boundaries. According to FEMA, for very flat areas where small changes in elevation can have a large impact on floodplain boundaries, LIDAR can provide the level of detail needed to accurately delineate the boundaries. Communities can also use detailed digital elevation data for planning and land development purposes. FEMA expects that LIDAR will be the primary technology used to acquire new digital elevation data for Risk MAP.

Figure 4: Light Detection and Ranging Technology Used to Generate Digital Elevation Data

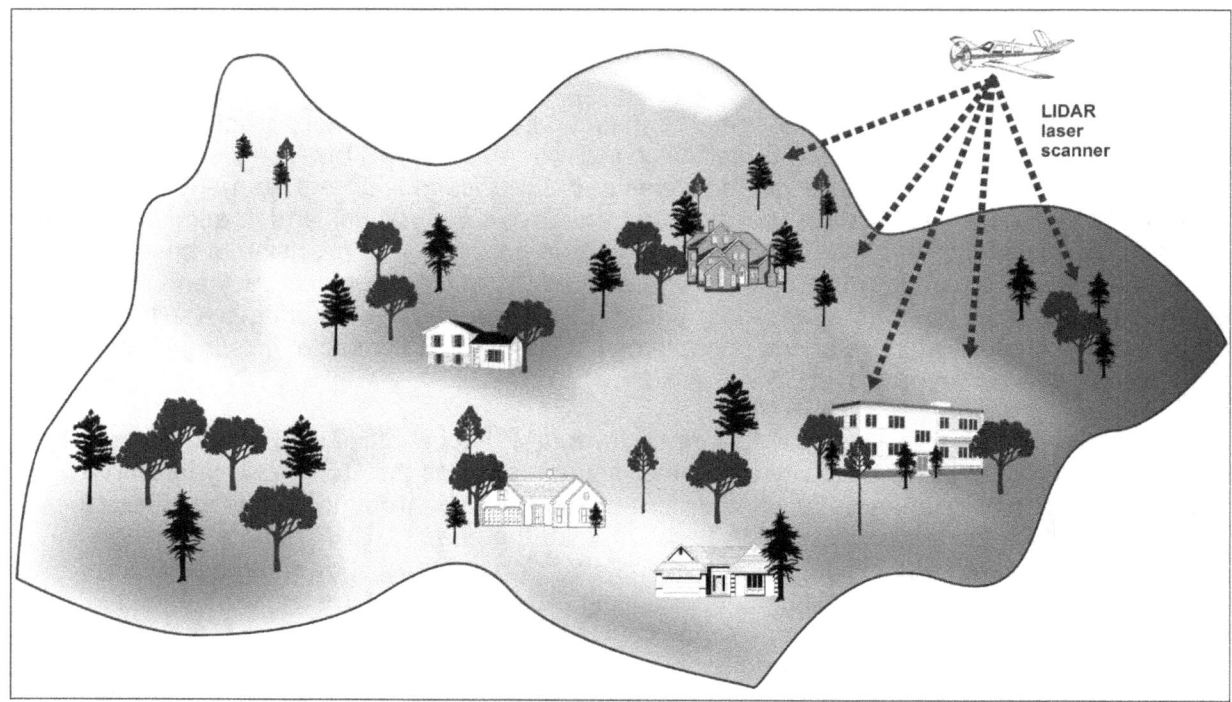

Source: GAO analysis of FEMA data; Art Explosion (images).

Our 2010 report also described challenges FEMA faced in implementing standards to ensure map accuracy.[104] For example, we found that FEMA's assessment of FBS compliance did not reflect the quality of topographic data or the level of detail used in creating the maps. Thus, two maps using topographical data of widely varying accuracy and currency, and based on studies of different levels of detail, could both be considered FBS-compliant as long as the base flood elevation and floodplain boundaries were consistent with the topographic data used in each study. We also concluded that one of the three elements of the NVUE standard had not been fully implemented. More specifically, draft guidance on how to validate data proved ineffective because it could be interpreted in different ways and because mapping contractors used different methodologies, according to FEMA officials and contractors who oversaw NVUE data collection and internal controls during the Map Modernization program.[105] Contractors had been using this guidance, issued in the form of checklists, to determine if enough changes had occurred in an area to render existing topographical data invalid, until FEMA determined that the process was not acceptable. As a result, validation of existing data was discontinued until uniform guidance could be developed in 2011, leaving only new and updated data as NVUE-compliant.

---

[104]GAO-11-17.

[105]Under Risk MAP, FEMA's goal is to achieve an NVUE compliance rate of 80 percent, meaning 80 percent of the nation's stream miles would be mapped using new or updated engineering analysis. Validating existing data could assist FEMA in reaching this compliance goal.

To address our 2010 report's recommendations for improving the accuracy of flood maps, FEMA took a number of steps.[106] For example, to more accurately assess FBS compliance, FEMA issued guidance that included FBS compliance requirements that were based on a flood study's level of detail. Successful implementation of this guidance could enable FEMA to use FBS data as a more meaningful measure of map accuracy and to enhance reporting on FBS compliance. Additionally, to help FEMA more fully implement the NVUE standard, the agency issued guidance for validating existing engineering data and procedures to implement a full validation assessment of the flood map inventory. By following this guidance, FEMA could be better able to verify the validity of existing engineering data prior to the initiation of a new or revised flood study. The 2014 Act contains provisions related to map accuracy. For example, it requires FEMA to implement a flood mapping program, after review by TMAC, that results in technically credible flood hazard data in all areas for which FIRMS are prepared or updated.[107]

Finally, we noted in 2013 and previous reports that FEMA historically has not been authorized to account for long-term erosion—which results from climate change and rising sea levels—when updating flood maps used to set premium rates for NFIP.[108] Not accurately reflecting the actual risk of flooding increases the likelihood that even full-risk premiums will not cover future losses and adds to concerns about NFIP's financial stability. In 2011 we suggested that Congress authorize NFIP to account for long-term flood erosion in its flood maps.[109] As previously noted, the Biggert-Waters Act required FEMA to create a new TMAC. According to the act, TMAC must issue a report with recommendations on how to ensure that (1) FIRMs incorporate the best available climate science and (2) FEMA uses the best available methodology to consider the impact of rising sea levels and future development on flood risk.[110] Additionally, the act requires FEMA to incorporate the report's findings into updates to flood maps.

---

[106]Our recommendations were based on key attributes of successful performance measures. See GAO, *Tax Administration: IRS Needs to Further Refine Its Tax Filing Season Performance Measures*, GAO-03-143 (Washington, D.C.: Nov. 22, 2002).

[107]Pub. L. No. 113-89, § 17.

[108]*GAO, High-Risk Series: An Update*, GAO-13-283 (Washington, D.C.: Feb. 14, 2013).

[109]The purpose of flood maps is to accurately estimate the likelihood of flooding in specific areas given certain characteristics including elevation and topography. See GAO, *FEMA: Action Needed to Improve Administration of the National Flood Insurance Program*, GAO-11-297 (Washington, D.C.: June 9, 2011).

[110]As previously noted, this report was due by July 6, 2013, but FEMA was in the process of establishing TMAC as of February 2014.

Enclosure V: Flood Mitigation

Background

FEMA supports a variety of flood mitigation activities that are designed to reduce flood risk and the financial exposure of NFIP. A variety of mitigation activities exist that can reduce the risk of losses from flooding. These activities, which are mostly implemented at the state and local level, include hazard mitigation planning; the adoption and enforcement of floodplain management regulations and building codes; and the use of hazard control structures such as levees, dams, and floodwalls or natural protective features such as wetlands and dunes. Additionally, property-level mitigation options include elevating a building to or above the area's base flood elevation (see fig. 5), relocating the building to an area of less flood risk, or purchasing and demolishing the building and turning the property into green space.[111]

Figure 5: Elevating a House to Mitigate against Flood Damage

Source: FEMA.

Communities Play a Key Role in Mitigating Flood Risk

Communities mitigate flood risk through planning and enforcement. When communities join NFIP, they must adopt and enforce floodplain management regulations and enforce building codes, including those regulating where structures may be built within the floodplain. Communities must also verify that substantially flood-damaged properties are repaired to reflect the flood risk. We reported in 2007 that according to a FEMA estimate, $1.2 billion in flood losses are avoided annually because of community implementation of NFIP's floodplain management requirements.[112]

---

[111]The base flood elevation is the elevation relative to mean sea level at which there is a 1 percent chance of floodwaters rising in a given year. The base flood elevation within a community can change throughout the floodplain.

[112]GAO, *Natural Hazard Mitigation: Various Mitigation Efforts Exist, but Federal Efforts Do Not Provide a Comprehensive Strategic Framework,* GAO-07-403 (Washington, D.C.: Aug. 22, 2007).

We also found that insurance premium discounts can promote mitigation by rewarding property owners for actions taken by communities to reduce the effects of flooding. For example, the NFIP Community Rating System (CRS) provides discounts on flood insurance for property owners in communities that establish floodplain management programs that go beyond NFIP's minimum requirements. Depending on the level of activities that communities undertake in four areas—public information, mapping and regulatory activities, flood damage reduction, and flood preparedness—communities are categorized into 1 of 10 CRS classes. A Class 1 rating provides the largest flood insurance premium reduction (45 percent), while a community with a Class 10 rating receives no insurance premium reduction. FEMA officials stated that the CRS insurance discounts are an effective means of encouraging communities that participate in NFIP to undertake more aggressive flood mitigation. Although few communities participate in CRS, they represent a substantial percentage of NFIP policies—according to FEMA about 67 percent as of July 2012.

FEMA's Mitigation Programs Reduce Risk and Financial Exposure, but Program Demand Exceeds Resources

FEMA mitigates flood risk through a number of programs, which generally have cost-sharing requirements—that is, FEMA pays part of the cost, and the rest must come from nonfederal sources. We have concluded in several previous reports, including a report from 2013, that one option for reducing flood risk and financial exposure is increasing mitigation efforts.[113] The cost of mitigation can be high, but according to FEMA one dollar spent on hazard mitigation provides about two to three dollars in future benefits. However, the demand for mitigation funds currently exceeds appropriated amounts. For example, FEMA officials told us that the agency had received applications for $304 million in Flood Mitigation Assistance—FEMA's primary predisaster mitigation program—in 2013, more than twice the appropriations received for the program that year.

As shown in table 5, FEMA mitigates risk before and after disasters. The Flood Mitigation Assistance and the Pre-Disaster Mitigation programs fund predisaster mitigation, while the Hazard Mitigation Grant program and Increased Cost of Compliance program fund postdisaster mitigation. Funds from the Increased Cost of Compliance program and some of the Flood Mitigation Assistance program funds go directly to property owners, while funds from the other programs generally flow through states and localities. The Biggert-Waters Act eliminated two mitigation programs for repetitive and severe repetitive loss properties.[114] According to FEMA

---

[113]GAO, *Flood Insurance: Options for Addressing the Financial Impact of Subsidized Premium Rates on the National Flood Insurance Program*, GAO-09-20 (Washington, D.C.: Nov. 14, 2008), *Flood Insurance: Public Policy Goals Provide a Framework for Reform*, GAO-11-670T (Washington, D.C.: June 23, 2011), and *Flood Insurance: More Information Needed on Subsidized Properties*, GAO-13-607 (Washington, D.C.: July 3, 2013).

[114]Pub. L. No. 112-141, §100225(b)-(c), 126 Stat. 405, 941 (2012). In the context of mitigation programs, FEMA defines a repetitive loss property as a structure that (1) incurred flood-related damage on two occasions, in which the cost of repair, on average, equaled or exceeded 25 percent of the market value of the structure at the time of each flood event; and (2) at the time of the second incidence of flood-related damage, had a flood insurance contract that contained increased cost of compliance coverage. In the mitigation context, FEMA defines a severe repetitive loss property as a structure that has incurred flood-related damage and for which (1) four or more separate claim payments were made and each claim exceeded $5,000 and the cumulative claim amount exceeded $20,000; or (2) at least two separate claim payments were made and the cumulative claim amount exceeded the market value of the structure.

officials, portions of these programs were incorporated into the Flood Mitigation Assistance program and the overall funding remained the same. As a result of this change, applications for Flood Mitigation Assistance grants that address repetitive or severe repetitive loss properties are given additional weight during the application rating process. To further encourage mitigation for these properties, the act increases the federal portion of mitigation costs.[115] FEMA pays up to 100 percent of the mitigation costs for severe repetitive loss properties, up to 90 percent for repetitive loss properties, and up to 75 percent for all other mitigation projects. Prior to the act, the federal portion was 75 percent regardless of a property's flood history. FEMA officials said that combining the programs simplified the application process and program administration. The Biggert-Waters Act made additional changes to the mitigation programs.[116] Specifically, demolition and rebuilding efforts that meet specific criteria are now an eligible mitigation method, and the use of mitigation funds is limited to activities that are consistent with FEMA-approved mitigation plans. Further, the 2014 Act requires FEMA to establish guidelines for property owners that provide alternative methods of mitigation, other than building elevation, to reduce flood risk to residential buildings that cannot be elevated due to their structural characteristics.[117]

---

[115]Pub. L. No. 112-141, §100225, 126 Stat. 405, 938 (2012).

[116]Pub. L. No. 112-141, §100205, 100225(a), 126 Stat. 405, 917, 938 (2012).

[117]Pub. L. No. 113-89, §26.

Table 5: FEMA's Mitigation Programs

Program	Original authority	Purpose and funding	Planning requirement	Cost-share requirement
Flood Mitigation Assistance	Section 1366 of the National Flood Insurance Act of 1968, as added by the National Flood Insurance Reform Act of 1994	To implement cost-effective measures that reduce or eliminate the long-term risk of flood damage to buildings, manufactured homes, and other structures insured under NFIP. Appropriation for fiscal year 2013 was $120 million.	FEMA-approved state and local flood mitigation plans prior to award.	Up to 100 percent in federal funds for severe repetitive loss properties, up to 90 percent for repetitive loss properties, and up to 75 percent for all other mitigation projects. Any remaining percentage must come from nonfederal funds.
Hazard Mitigation Grant	Section 404 of the Robert T. Stafford Disaster Relief and Emergency Relief Act	To provide funds to states, territories, Indian tribal governments, and communities to reduce or eliminate future risks to lives and property from natural hazards, in accordance with identified priorities. Funding is included in postdisaster appropriations.[a]	FEMA-approved state and local mitigation plans prior to award.	Up to 75 percent in federal funds, with a minimum of 25 percent in nonfederal funds. Nonfederal contribution does not need to be in cash; in-kind services or materials may be used.
Pre-Disaster Mitigation	Title I of the Disaster Mitigation Act of 2000	To provide funds to states, territories, Indian tribal governments, and communities for hazard mitigation planning and the implementation of predisaster mitigation projects. Appropriation for fiscal year 2013 was $25 million.	FEMA-approved state and local/tribal standard or enhanced hazard mitigation plans prior to award.	Up to 75 percent in federal funds, with a minimum of 25 percent in nonfederal funds, although small, impoverished communities may be eligible for up to a 90 percent federal cost-share.
Increased Cost of Compliance Coverage	Section 1304 of the NFIA of 1968, as amended by the National Flood Insurance Reform Act of 1994	To provide up to $30,000 to policyholders to help cover the cost of mitigation measures for flood-damaged properties. This amount is in addition to building coverage under the standard flood insurance policy. Funded from premiums collected.[b]	Not applicable.	No cost-share requirement. However, program funds may be used as nonfederal matching funds in concert with FEMA mitigation grants.

Source: FEMA and the Biggert-Waters Act.

[a]After flood disasters, Congress may provide financial assistance to a state or county. Funding for the Hazard Mitigation Grant Program is included in this funding.

[b]As part of the claim process, property owners can mitigate as part of the repair process.

FEMA Has Taken Steps to Improve Collaboration on Mitigation Activities and Track Outcomes

We reported in 2007 on impediments to the implementation of mitigation activities and collaborative efforts to promote mitigation.[118] We found that mitigation activities were often

---

[118]GAO-07-403.

constrained by conflicting local interests, cost concerns, and a lack of public awareness of the risks of natural hazards and the importance of mitigation. Additionally, we found that successful mitigation efforts require collaboration among federal, state, and local government agencies and a variety of nongovernmental entities, because mitigation activities are implemented at the state and local levels. Given FEMA's role in leading emergency management efforts, our 2007 report recommended that FEMA, in consultation with other federal agencies, develop and maintain a national comprehensive strategic framework for mitigation that incorporated both pre- and postdisaster mitigation efforts.[119] We recommended that the framework include items such as common mitigation goals; performance measures and reporting requirements; the role of specific activities in the overall framework; and the roles and responsibilities of federal, state, and local agencies and nongovernmental stakeholders. Consistent with our recommendation, FEMA established a national preparedness goal citing the importance of predisaster efforts. The goal also states that a community's ability to accelerate the recovery process begins with its predisaster preparedness efforts, including mitigation and planning for and building capacity for disaster recovery. Additionally FEMA developed a Mitigation Framework addressing how the nation will coordinate core mitigation capabilities to reduce loss of life and property by lessening the impact of disasters. The framework cites the importance of coordination and including the private and public sectors, nonprofits, and individuals in mitigation efforts.

We found in 2008 that, contrary to federal internal control standards for recording transactions, FEMA did not properly track the number of properties purchased through its mitigation programs.[120] This deficiency limits FEMA's ability to accurately assess or report on the effectiveness of its mitigation efforts. The amounts available for mitigation activities such as the purchase and demolition of flood-damaged properties, increased for NFIP's mitigation programs in 2006. Although properties had been purchased through these programs, we found that FEMA did not know the total number of properties purchased because of a lack of reporting requirements and information system limitations that hampered assessments of the programs. For example, we found that FEMA's grants management system did not allow for the electronic capture of data on property acquisitions. These limitations mean that FEMA management cannot readily determine the effectiveness of the mitigation programs or the number of acquisitions, as buying properties is a key means of reducing or eliminating future insurance claims. We recommended that FEMA: (1) establish written guidance for its regional offices to better ensure consistent and timely recording of property acquisition data and (2) establish a method to track real-time property acquisitions for NFIP-funded mitigation programs. FEMA issued revised reporting requirements in July 2013 to its regional offices but, as of December 2013, did not have information on the offices' adherence to these requirements.

---

[119]More specifically, the Post-Katrina Emergency Reform Act of 2006 defined FEMA's primary mission as reducing the loss of life and property "by leading and supporting the nation in a risk-based comprehensive emergency management system of preparedness, protection, response, recovery, and mitigation." See Pub. L. No. 109-295, § 601, 120 Stat. 1355, 1396 (2006) (codified as 6 U.S.C. § 313).

[120]GAO, *National Flood Insurance Program: Financial Challenges Underscore Need for Improved Oversight of Mitigation Programs and Key Contacts*, GAO-08-437 (Washington, D.C.: June 16, 2008).

Enclosure VI: Administration and Oversight

Background

FEMA includes the Federal Insurance and Mitigation Administration (FIMA), which administers NFIP. FIMA relies extensively on contractors and private insurance companies to perform critical functions. For example, one contractor acts as the agency's Bureau and Statistical Agent (BSA), which collects and reports on all NFIP financial and statistical data. FIMA also relies heavily on Write-Your-Own (WYO) insurance companies to sell and service flood insurance policies and report policy and claims information to BSA. As of January 2014, there were 84 companies participating in the WYO program. DHS provides management direction by issuing guidance and working to integrate its various management processes, systems, and staff within and across management areas.

FEMA Faces Ongoing Challenges in Strategic and Human Capital Planning

In 2011, we found that FEMA's agencywide strategic plan for fiscal years 2011 through 2014 did not clearly lay out how NFIP's mission and activities fit within FEMA's own goals and objectives.[121] FEMA officials told us that the agency chose not to prescribe goals and objectives for specific programs in its strategic plan in order to allow for the flexibility FEMA needs as it responds to emergencies. At the time of our 2011 review, FIMA officials told us that they were developing a strategy for mitigation and insurance, but did not provide a specific timeline for completing or implementing the plan and did not provide details of what it might include. Our 2011 report also concluded that while FIMA officials planned to include long-term goals and objectives in a forthcoming strategic plan, until the plan was completed and effectively implemented, FIMA would continue to be challenged by a lack of strategic focus and direction. FIMA officials said that they had relied on other documents for strategic guidance, including FEMA- and DHS-level guidance, as well as on the agency's general mission—managing risks from all natural hazards to help free America from the burden of such disasters. Further, our 2011 report concluded that without specific agency- or program-level goals, FIMA could not ensure that any performance measures it developed for NFIP could properly and adequately measure the program's success.

Given the importance of strategic planning to agency management, we recommended that FEMA provide direction for FIMA operations.[122] In response, FEMA completed a multiyear planning document in November 2012 that laid out FEMA's strategic direction and plans for incorporating FIMA's strategic goals within FEMA's goals. It also sets specific expectations for the completion and regular updating of strategic planning documents, including performance goals. FEMA will need to fully implement this guidance to ensure that its next strategic plan provides appropriate direction for NFIP's mission and activities.

In our 2011 report, we also found that FEMA lacked a strategic human capital plan that met statutory requirements and that addressed the agency's human capital challenges, including those affecting NFIP. The Post-Katrina Emergency Management Reform Act of 2006

---

[121]GAO-11-297.

[122]More specifically, the basis for our recommendations was that an agency's strategic planning effort is the most important element in results-oriented management and serves as the foundation for defining what the agency seeks to accomplish, identifying strategies to achieve desired results, and determining how well it succeeds in reaching its goals and objectives.

(PKEMRA) required FEMA to develop a strategic human capital plan that included an assessment of (1) the critical skills and competencies that would be needed in the workforce during the 10-year period after the law was enacted; (2) the skills and competencies of the FEMA workforce and projected trends in that workforce based on the expected losses due to retirement and other attrition; and (3) staffing levels for each category of employee and gaps that should be addressed to ensure that FEMA has continued access to the necessary critical skills and competencies. In addition, PKEMRA required FEMA to develop a Plan of Action to address gaps in critical skills and competencies, including:

- specific goals and objectives for recruiting and retaining employees, such as recruitment and retention bonuses;

- specific strategies and program objectives to develop, train, deploy, compensate, motivate, and retain employees; and

- specific strategies for recruiting staff with experience serving in multiple state agencies responsible for emergency management.

While FEMA developed a 2008-2012 strategic human capital plan and an action plan in response to PKEMRA, we found that the plans did not meet all of the act's requirements. For example, they did not contain specific strategies and program objectives to motivate, deploy, and retain employees, among other things. We have concluded in previous work that agencies should develop human capital strategies—including succession planning, training, and staff development—to eliminate gaps between current skills and competencies needed for mission success.[123] Our 2011 report recommended that FEMA develop a comprehensive workforce plan in accordance with PKEMRA that identified agency staffing and skills requirements, addressed turnover and staff vacancies, and analyzed FEMA's use of contractors. FEMA has taken some steps to implement these recommendations, such as aligning its human capital strategy with the Quadrennial Homeland Security Review and analyzing staffing resources and staffing gaps through a workload analysis tool.[124] According to FEMA officials, this analysis is under management review for final approval. The officials also noted that FEMA was continuing to incorporate into its workforce analysis the workload changes precipitated by the Biggert-Waters Act.

In our 2011 report, we also found that neither FEMA nor FIMA had a plan to help ensure consistent day-to-day operations when staff were deployed to federally declared disasters. Without such a plan, FEMA faces the risk that some critical day-to-day functions might not be performed while staff are deployed, limiting the agency's ability to provide the necessary support for disaster relief missions. FEMA staff can be deployed for weeks or months and, during that time, are often performing duties in the field that take them away from their day-to-day responsibilities. According to a 2010 study by the Homeland Security Studies and Analysis Institute, an independent research center funded by the federal government, FEMA staff found

---

[123]These strategies are based on lessons learned from leading organizations. See GAO, *Human Capital: Key Principles for Effective Strategic Workforce Planning*, GAO-04-39 (Washington, D.C.: Dec. 11, 2003), and *Budget Issues: FEMA Needs Adequate Data, Plans, and Systems to Effectively Manage Resources for Day-to-Day Operations*, GAO-07-139 (Washington, D.C.: Jan. 19, 2007).

[124]The Quadrennial Homeland Security Review outlines a strategic framework to guide the activities of participants in homeland security toward a common end. According to FEMA, this document describes the vision for a secure homeland, specifies key mission priorities, outlines goals for each of those mission areas, and lays the groundwork for subsequent steps.

that operating normally during and immediately after a disaster was problematic due to staff deployment and an increased workload.[125] For this reason, business continuity planning is particularly important for the agency. FEMA took steps to address our recommendation to improve its continuity planning by identifying critical staff and key operations that needed to continue when staff were deployed to a disaster and determining how operations would continue during such periods.[126]

FEMA Has Generally Addressed Weaknesses in Its Financial Management Processes

We have reported that FEMA faced challenges in its financial reporting process and oversight structures, creating the risk of inaccurate or incomplete NFIP financial information. For example, in 2009 we found that:

- internal control weaknesses had impaired FEMA's ability to maintain transaction-level accountability;

- FEMA's broader oversight structures such as WYO company audits, the triennial operational reviews of WYOs, and FEMA's claims reinspection program were limited in their effectiveness; and

- FEMA's initiative to resolve specific internal control weaknesses and improve the overall NFIP control environment since the 2005 Gulf Coast hurricanes had done little to address many of the NFIP financial data deficiencies highlighted by these catastrophic events.[127]

In our 2009 report, we made seven recommendations to improve NFIP's financial reporting process and strengthen compliance with federal internal control standards. At the time of our 2009 review, FEMA's internal controls over NFIP offered limited transaction-level accountability and assurances that financial reporting was accurate or that insurance company operations conformed to program requirements. FEMA addressed six of the recommendations by, among other things, verifying and validating through independent audits the reliability of financial information that WYOs insurers provided, establishing procedures for conducting claims operation reviews within 3-year time periods, and establishing and implementing procedures to select claims for reinspection. As of December 2013, FEMA had not addressed our remaining recommendation to improve transaction-level accountability by developing procedures for analyzing financial reports in relation to the transaction-level information that WYO companies submit for statistical purposes. Although FEMA has not developed procedures, an audit of FEMA's financial statements would achieve a similar result by verifying material amounts from WYO companies' summary reports. An audit of FEMA's financial statements is planned for fiscal year 2014 may address this recommendation.

---

[125]See Homeland Security Studies and Analysis Institute, *Federal Emergency Management Agency Workforce Baseline Assessment, Final Report;* (Arlington, Va.: Mar. 31, 2010).

[126]We made this recommendation based on the importance of business continuity management and deployment planning. The goal of business continuity planning management is to keep operations running in the event of a disruption to normal business practices. As a program, it includes activities such as planning, risk analysis, providing backup facilities, succession plans, and impact assessments.

[127]GAO-10-66.

FEMA Has Implemented Some Changes in Its Acquisitions Management Activities, but Needs to Complete Key Steps

We also found in 2011 that some FEMA investments have been funded despite not receiving adequate review or oversight. Most notably, acquisition management weaknesses led to the cancellation of NFIP's effort to modernization its flood policy and claims management system. The effort to modernize NFIP's flood policy and claims management system went forward without necessary reviews and failed after 7 years and an investment of $40 million.[128] Further, the $1 billion Risk MAP program, an effort begun in fiscal year 2009 to modernize flood mapping, was funded without receiving approval from an appropriate DHS review board.[129] As we also found in 2011, FEMA had identified weaknesses in its oversight and management of acquisitions, and DHS and FEMA had taken a number of steps to improve these functions.[130] However, because some of these steps were either recently implemented or are under development, the extent to which they will improve FEMA's oversight and management of acquisitions remains to be seen.

To better address DHS's acquisition oversight needs, the agency issued an interim acquisition directive in November 2008 and a final directive in January 2010.[131] The directive provides an overall policy and structure for acquisition management within DHS. It describes the acquisition review processes and the role of the Acquisition Review Board (FEMA's was established in July 2009), and outlines management procedures and responsibilities related to various aspects of acquisition.[132] In addition, in May 2011 FEMA published its own directive on the review of contracts that was consistent with the department directive, and also issued updated guidance in October 2011 that explains its acquisition process.[133]

Although our 2011 report recognized the actions FEMA was taking to improve its oversight and management of acquisitions—such as the January 2010 acquisition directive—it also found that FEMA's actions had either been recently implemented or were under development. Accordingly, we recommended that FEMA establish timelines for and complete the development and implementation of its revised acquisition process, including a rollout process with staff training and a mechanism to better ensure that all acquisitions underwent the necessary reviews. FEMA agreed with this recommendation, and FEMA officials stated that they had made progress in the area of acquisition management and planned to address the recommendation by October 2014. Officials stated that progress included filling the majority of positions for a team of qualified acquisition personnel, beginning the pilot phase of an electronic contract filing and monitoring system, and making progress in hiring experienced contracting officers to work at disaster sites.

---

[128]Enclosure VII on information management issues contains additional information on this system.

[129]GAO-11-297.

[130]GAO-11-297.

[131]DHS Acquisition Directive No. 102-01, Draft Version 1.9 (Nov. 7, 2008) and DHS Acquisition Management Directive No. 102-01, (Jan. 20, 2010).

[132]The Acquisition Review Board is a cross-component board within DHS that determines whether a proposed acquisition has met the requirements of key phases in the acquisition life-cycle framework and is able to proceed to the next phase and eventual full production and deployment.

[133]Federal Emergency Management Agency, Directive 143-4, May 24, 2011 and Federal Emergency Management Agency, *FEMA Acquisition Planning: A Guide to Preparing Acquisition Packages*, Version 2.0, Office of the Chief Procurement Officer, Mission Support Bureau, October 2011.

Completing these efforts will be critical to establishing a well-functioning acquisition management program.

FEMA Has Made Progress in Contractor Oversight, but Opportunities Exist for Further Improvement

In prior work, we identified a number of operational challenges that hindered FEMA's ability to effectively administer NFIP, including problems with the oversight of contractors responsible for performing key NFIP functions. However, our most recent review indicates that FEMA has made progress in developing and implementing its NFIP-related contract management policies and procedures.

We found in 2008 that a lack of monitoring records, an inconsistent application of procedures, and a lack of coordination diminished the effectiveness of FEMA's monitoring of NFIP-related contracts.[134] Our review of monitoring documentation for the BSA contract showed that FEMA did not consistently follow its own monitoring procedures for preparing, maintaining, and reviewing monitoring reports and was unable to provide copies of the majority of the monitoring reports we requested. Moreover, our 2008 review found that key FEMA offices responsible for addressing contractor deficiencies did not coordinate by sharing information or taking actions related to these deficiencies. We made several recommendations to help ensure compliance with monitoring procedures and more effective oversight of contractors performing key NFIP data collection, reporting, and insurance functions. FEMA addressed our recommendations through actions, such as monitoring contractors against specific performance standards, completing monitoring reports and uploading them into an information system in a timely manner, and implementing a process to review monthly contract monitoring reports.

In 2011, we described ongoing challenges that FEMA faced in the acquisition and oversight of its contractors, which are critical to NFIP.[135] Both Office of Chief Procurement Officer (OCPO) and FIMA officials said there had been communication challenges between contracting officers who were part of OCPO and Contracting Officer's Representatives (COR), who report to the contracting officers but also work in the program offices. OCPO officials said that many CORs were loyal to their program office and communicated with contracting officers only when a problem arose. FIMA officials said that contracting officers had at times been unresponsive to them, particularly when reporting contractor deficiencies.

In January 2014, we reported on FEMA's policies and procedures for monitoring NFIP contractors and the extent to which FEMA was following its monitoring procedures for the largest NFIP contractors.[136] We conducted this work in response to a mandate in the Biggert-Waters Act to review the three largest contractors used in administering NFIP. We concluded that FEMA had made progress in developing its contract management policies and procedures. Additionally, with some exceptions, we found that FEMA was generally following contract monitoring procedures for the three largest NFIP contractors. We also found some opportunity for further improvements and made recommendations designed to strengthen FEMA's quality

---

[134]GAO-08-437.

[135]GAO-11-297.

[136]GAO, *National Flood Insurance Program: Progress Made on Contract Management but Monitoring and Reporting Could Be Improved,* GAO-14-160 (Washington, D.C. Jan. 15, 2014).

assurance and contractor evaluation efforts.[137] FEMA concurred with our recommendations and stated that it expected to address them by the end of January 2014.

---

[137]We made these recommendations on the basis that the development of a quality assurance surveillance plan is a best practice and a key requirement identified in regulations and guidance. Moreover, federal and DHS regulations and FEMA contract management guidance require entry of contract performance information in the Contractor Performance Assessment Reporting System within certain time frames.

Enclosure VII: Information Management

Background

The Federal Insurance and Mitigation Administration (FIMA), which administers NFIP, receives information technology (IT) support from the agency's Office of Chief Information Officer (OCIO). This office's stated function is to assist FEMA offices in IT development and help ensure they follow the agency's established processes for implementing IT systems.

FEMA has IT systems for variety of purposes, including invoicing, debt collection, and financial management. A key system supporting FEMA's administration of NFIP is the flood insurance policy and claims processing system. FEMA's Bureau and Statistical Agent (BSA)—which serves as a liaison between the government and WYO insurance companies—uses this 30-year-old system to (1) collect data to determine flood insurance premium rates for specific properties, (2) collect data on claims made on properties that have had flood-related damage, (3) track the progress of policies and claims, and (4) prepare legislatively mandated reports for Congress.

FEMA Lacks Adequate Systems for Document and Financial Management

We found in 2011 that FEMA was a paper-based agency and had no centralized electronic document management system that would allow its administration, regional, and program offices—including FIMA—to easily access and store documents.[138] According to the National Archives and Records Administration, a record enters the document life cycle at its creation and remains in the system through its use, maintenance, and disposition.[139] Records enable and support an agency's ability to fulfill its mission. As a result, it is essential to take a systematic approach to effectively managing records. From a strategic perspective, agencies lacking effective records management policies and procedures can hinder their ability to respond swiftly to opportunities, events, incoming requests, and investigations and effectively implement policy.

FEMA officials told us they had not implemented a FEMA-wide system, even on an interim basis, because they were waiting for a decision from DHS on a centralized system. FEMA agreed with our recommendation to consider the costs and benefits of an interim document management system for FEMA while waiting for DHS to implement a DHS-wide system. However, as of February 2014, FEMA had not implemented this recommendation and DHS had not implemented a centralized document management system.

Our 2011 review also found that FEMA lacked effective and systematic procedures to fully ensure that it appropriately retained and managed its records. While DHS had an overall records management directive at the time of our review, FEMA's agency-specific guidance was outdated. For example, the guidance included direction on file cabinet sizes and the use of candles in file rooms but did not provide clear direction on electronic recordkeeping. On the basis of effective record management practices, we recommended that FEMA update its document management policies and procedures while waiting for DHS to implement a DHS-wide document management system. FEMA agreed with this recommendation and is updating

---

[138]GAO-11-297.

[139]The National Archives and Records Administration is an independent agency that oversees management of federal government records including presidential libraries and historic collections.

its existing document management practices. According to FEMA officials, when the practices are approved, they will be issued FEMA-wide.

Further, our 2011 report found that FEMA's financial management systems were out of date. According to FEMA staff, FEMA's systems for invoicing, travel management, and debt collection did not interface with FEMA's financial management system. As a result, staff had to manually enter data into FEMA's financial management system, a practice that was inefficient and could lead to errors. We also concluded that the lack of automated systems for budget formulation and execution created challenges. Our report found that FIMA was using a system of spreadsheets to formulate fiscal year budgets and to track overall budget expenditure and specific line-item expenses. Performing these key functions with spreadsheets can be problematic. For example, according to FIMA officials, when staff worked on multiple versions of spreadsheets, the spreadsheets could become corrupted and errors could be introduced. In addition, FIMA staff told us that they faced challenges with the paper-based tracking of requisition orders sent among departments. In order to determine what was approved or not approved in the system on a daily basis, staff had to manually track requisition packages through various offices. While FIMA had begun to implement an automated tracking system at the time of our 2011 review, according to FEMA staff the process was delayed by IT challenges, including a lack of server capacity.

Finally, in our 2011 report, we found that FEMA's outdated financial management systems and processes left unliquidated obligations unresolved.[140] Specifically, we found that an audit of DHS's financial statements had identified material weaknesses in this area. As of March 2011, FEMA had a total of $3.3 million in unliquidated obligations for NFIP-related funds that had been inactive for at least 5 years. A FEMA official said about $3.0 million of these funds could have potentially been deobligated and made available for other allowable purposes. According to Standards for Internal Control in the Federal Government, transactions should be promptly recorded and clearly documented to maintain their relevance and value to management in controlling operations and making decisions.[141] This guidance applies to the entire process or life cycle of a transaction or event, from initiation and authorization through its final classification in summary records. Thus, we recommended that FEMA regularly review unliquidated obligations within NFIP-related funds. FEMA addressed this recommendation by revising guidance for managing open obligations and providing documentation that the new guidance was being followed.

Information Systems Were Developed without Full Collaboration among Agency Offices

In our 2011 report, we found that collaboration among offices within FEMA that were responsible for administering NFIP had at times been ineffective, leading to challenges in effectively carrying out some key functions.[142] In particular, our report described limited collaboration between FIMA and OCIO in developing IT systems. For example, FIMA officials said they had experienced difficulty in the past getting timely approvals from OCIO for IT

---

[140]Obligations are definite commitments that create a legal liability of the government for the payment of goods and services ordered or received. Unliquidated obligations refer to the value of goods and services ordered and obligated but not yet delivered.

[141]GAO/AIMD-00-21.3.1.

[142]GAO-11-297.

programs and contracts for NFIP and had sought ways to streamline the process, including using contractors rather than OCIO staff. OCIO officials acknowledged that some communication problems existed and said they were aware of FIMA's concerns. OCIO's primary concern, however, was that at times FIMA would perform IT functions independently from OCIO. OCIO believed that involving OCIO would help streamline IT development.

In our prior work, we have identified key practices that agencies can use to enhance and sustain their collaboration efforts, including agreeing on roles and responsibilities and establishing mutually reinforcing or joint strategies.[143] On the basis of those practices, we recommended that FEMA develop protocols to encourage and monitor collaboration between FIMA and relevant support offices, including those for information technology. FEMA agreed with this recommendation and in response the agency's Mission Support Bureau—which provides administrative and management support to FIMA—said it was in the process of meeting with FEMA program offices to better understand their needs and encourage collaboration. FEMA expects to have completed meetings with relevant offices by the end of the first quarter of fiscal year 2014.

FEMA Has Taken Steps to Better Manage System Development, but Lacks a Modern Policy and Claims System

In our 2013 High-Risk Series update and in other reports, we found that FEMA had faced problems in modernizing NFIP's insurance policy and claims management system.[144] As previously noted, FEMA's BSA relies on a flood insurance management system from the 1980s to manage the flood policy and claims information that it obtains from insurance companies. This system is difficult and costly to maintain and provides only limited access to NFIP data. It consists of over 70 interfaced applications that use monthly tape and batch submissions of policy and claims data from insurance companies. According to FEMA officials, this system is neither efficient nor effective and does not adequately support the program's mission needs. We testified in 2010 that identifying and correcting errors in submissions required between 30 days and 6 months and that the general claims processing cycle itself took 2 to 3 months.[145]

In a 2011 report, we described the cancellation of a project to modernize NFIP's flood insurance policy and claims processing system.[146] Despite having invested roughly $40 million over 7 years, FEMA cancelled development of the Next Generation Flood Management System (NextGen) in November 2009 because testing showed that the system did not meet user expectations. We concluded that NFIP would have to rely on its legacy system for an unspecified period of time and that its ability to manage its flood insurance operations would continue to be hampered by the legacy system's limitations. Our 2011 report also observed that any further attempts to modernize the program's existing system would have to recognize the root causes of NextGen's failure, which include FEMA's and DHS's not providing sufficient

---

[143]See GAO, *Results-Oriented Government: Practices That Can Help Enhance and Sustain Collaboration among Federal Agencies*, GAO-06-15 (Washington, D.C.: Oct. 21, 2005).

[144]GAO-13-283.

[145]GAO, *National Flood Insurance Program: Continued Actions Needed to Address Financial and Operational Issues*, GAO-10-1063T (Washington, D.C.: Apr. 21, 2010).

[146]GAO-11-297.

oversight of the project and weaknesses in several key system acquisition areas. FEMA's OCIO initiated an evaluation to determine what, if anything, associated with NextGen could be salvaged. According to FEMA officials, the results of the evaluation were being reviewed within FEMA management as of March 2014.

To improve the usefulness and reliability of NFIP's flood insurance policy and claims processing system, we recommended that DHS direct the DHS Deputy Secretary, as the Chair of DHS's Acquisition Review Board, to provide regular oversight of FEMA's next attempt to modernize the system.[147] In response, FEMA established an NFIP steering committee that is responsible for overseeing FEMA's next attempt to modernize the system. The steering committee meets regularly to discuss the current status of the legacy system as well as modernization efforts. We also recommended that the FEMA Administrator ensure that FEMA's Chief Information Officer apply lessons learned from the NextGen experience to future efforts. FEMA cancelled NextGen because of weaknesses in several key system acquisition areas, including poorly defined and managed requirements.[148] To address this recommendation, FEMA has

- created clear system requirements and involved key stakeholders in the evaluation of systems on an ongoing basis,
- documented requirements for key test events and created a template for documenting test results,
- created a process for identification and mitigation of project risks, and
- created an NFIP IT project management office staffed with two deputy program executives hired from the private sector, each with significant IT experience.

These are positive steps, but FEMA must follow through on them to ensure that its next flood insurance policy and claims processing system fully supports mission needs.

---

[147]We based this recommendation, in part, on criteria we developed in prior work, which found that successfully acquiring IT systems required the oversight and informed decision making of a senior-level investment review board. See GAO, *Homeland Security: Despite Progress, DHS Continues to Be Challenged in Managing Its Multi-Billion Dollar Annual Investment in Large-Scale Information Technology Systems*, GAO-09-1002T (Washington, D.C.: Sept. 15, 2009); *Homeland Security: Progress Continues, but Challenges Remain on Department's Management of Information Technology*, GAO-06-598T (Washington, D.C.: Mar. 29, 2006); and *Business Systems Modernization: Department of the Navy Needs to Establish Management Structure and Fully Define Policies and Procedures for Institutionally Managing Investments*, GAO-08-53 (Washington, D.C.: Oct. 31, 2007).

[148]Well-defined requirements are a cornerstone of effective system acquisition. According to recognized guidance, documenting and implementing a disciplined process for developing and defining requirements can help reduce the risk of developing a system that does not perform as intended and does not meet user needs. See Carnegie Mellon Software Engineering Institute, *Capability Maturity Model® Integration for Development, Version 1.2* (Pittsburgh, Penn.: Aug. 2006). The Capability Maturity Model® Integration for Development (CMMI), developed by the Software Engineering Institute of Carnegie Mellon University, defines key practices that are recognized hallmarks for successful organizations that, if effectively implemented, can greatly increase the chances of successfully developing and acquiring software and systems.

Enclosure VIII: Status of NFIP Recommendations, February 2014

The following table summarizes the status of NFIP audit recommendations we have made since 2008. We classify each recommendation as either open (the agency has either not taken or completed steps to implement the recommendation) or closed-implemented. The recommendations are listed by report.

Table 6: Status of Recent GAO Recommendations Concerning NFIP, February 2014

Recommendations	Status
National Flood Insurance Program: Progress Made on Contract Management but Monitoring and Reporting Could Be Improved: GAO-14-160, January 15, 2014	
Determine the extent to which quality assurance surveillance plans have not been developed for FEMA contracts; identify the reasons why quality assurance surveillance plans were not developed; and develop additional actions as needed to address the reasons to help ensure that quality assurance surveillance plans are developed for its future awards.	Open
Determine the extent to which the Contractor Performance Assessment Reporting System (CPARS) assessments have not been completed for FEMA contracts; identify the reasons why CPARS assessments were not completed; and develop additional actions as needed to address the reasons to help ensure that assessments (ratings) for FEMA contractors are reported in CPARS on a timely and consistent basis.	Open
Flood Insurance: More Information Needed on Subsidized Properties: GAO-13-607, July 3, 2013	
To establish full-risk rates for properties with previously subsidized rates, develop and implement a plan, including a timeline, to obtain needed elevation information as soon as practicable.	Open
Flood Insurance: Participation of Indian Tribes in Federal and Private Programs: GAO-13-226, January 4, 2013	
Examine the feasibility of making mapping of tribal lands a higher priority.	Open
FEMA: Action Needed to Improve Administration of the National Flood Insurance Program: GAO-11-297, June 9, 2011	
Provide strategic direction and guidance to the process for developing a comprehensive strategy for Federal Insurance and Mitigation Administration (FIMA) operations; establish a firm time frame for and complete the development of this strategy; and take steps to ensure that this strategy has appropriate performance goals and measures to track NFIP's progress.	Closed-Implemented
Develop a comprehensive workforce plan according to the Post Katrina Emergency Management Reform Act of 2006 that identifies agency staffing and skills requirements, addresses turnover and staff vacancies, and analyzes FEMA's use of contractors.	Open
Develop guidance for continuing operations when staff are deployed to respond to federal disasters and direct FIMA to develop such a plan.	Closed-Implemented
Develop protocols to encourage and monitor collaboration between FIMA and relevant support offices, including those for information technology, acquisition management, and financial management.	Open
Consider the costs and benefits of implementing an interim system for FEMA and updating its document management policies and procedures while waiting for the Department of Homeland Security (DHS) to implement an agencywide electronic document management system.	Open
Ensure that FEMA regularly reviews unliquidated obligations within NFIP-related funds.	Closed-Implemented
Establish timelines for and complete the development and implementation of FEMA's revised acquisition process, in line with DHS Acquisition Directive 102-01, including a rollout process with staff training and a mechanism to better ensure that all acquisitions undergo the necessary reviews.	Open

Ensure that FEMA Mission Support's business process improvement efforts are expeditiously completed.	Open
Provide regular oversight of FEMA's next attempt to modernize this system.	Closed-Implemented
Apply lessons learned from the Next Generation Flood Insurance Management System (NextGen) experience to the next modernization attempt. At a minimum, this effort should ensure that (1) all levels of system requirements are complete and clear and that key stakeholders are adequately involved in requirements development and management, (2) key test events are effectively planned and executed and problems identified during testing effectively managed, (3) project risks are proactively identified and mitigated, and (4) project office staffing needs are properly assessed and met.	Closed-Implemented
FEMA Flood Maps: Some Standards and Processes in Place to Promote Map Accuracy and Outreach, but Opportunities Exist to Address Implementation Challenges: GAO-11-17, December 2, 2010	
Establish separate measures and collect data needed to assess compliance with the Floodplain Boundary Standard for detailed and approximate flood studies.	Closed-Implemented
Establish uniform guidance for the validation of existing engineering data to help FEMA fully implement the New, Validated, or Updated Engineering standard and provide a basis for mapping partners to validate flood hazard data.	Closed-Implemented
Implement probability sampling during the independent verification and validation (IV&V) audit process to the extent that the benefits outweigh the costs, to ensure that the results are generalizable for decision making.	Closed-Implemented
Transfer the IV&V audit process duties back to an independent entity to help ensure impartiality.	Closed-Implemented
Adopt a systematic approach to IV&V data collection, so FEMA can better track map quality issues, more easily analyze the data, and adopt a corrective action plan.	Closed-Implemented
Establish a mechanism to better ensure compliance with the documentation requirements of public notification regulations.	Closed-Implemented
Collect and analyze data on appeals and protests, including those on ineligible appeals, to the extent that the benefits outweigh the costs.	Closed-Implemented
Issue guidance to mapping stakeholders to standardize the process for analyzing appeals and protests and submitting these data to FEMA.	Closed-Implemented
Establish performance goals and measures for promoting public acceptance of flood maps.	Closed-Implemented
Develop a reporting structure for regions to use to identify resources needed to conduct flood mapping outreach activities, and implement a risk-based approach to allocate outreach resources.	Closed-Implemented
Leverage, as appropriate, existing FloodSmart marketing resources and expertise to help increase public acceptance of flood maps.	Closed-Implemented
Financial Management: Improvements Needed in National Flood Insurance Program's Financial Controls and Oversight: GAO-10-66, December 22, 2009	
Augment NFIP policies to require the Bureau and Statistical Agent (BSA) to develop procedures to analyze financial reports in relation to the transaction-level information that Write-Your-Own (WYO) companies submit for statistical purposes.	Open
Revise required internal control activities for BSA to provide for verifying and validating the reliability of WYO-reported financial information based upon a review of a sample of the underlying transactions or events, or obtain verification that these objectives have been met through independent audits of the WYO companies.	Closed-Implemented
Determine the feasibility of integrating and streamlining numerous existing NFIP financial reporting processes to reduce the risk of errors inherent in the manual recording of accounting transactions into multiple systems.	Closed-Implemented

Establish and implement procedures to require reviewing available information such as the results of biennial audits, operational reviews, and claim reinspections to determine whether the targeted audits for cause managerial tool should be used.	Closed-Implemented
Establish and implement procedures to require maintaining and considering current information from an independent source regarding state audit results to gather pertinent information such as customer service issues and inform determinations about when to conduct audits for cause.	Closed-Implemented
Establish and implement procedures to schedule and conduct all required operational reviews within the prescribed 3-year period.	Closed-Implemented
Establish and implement procedures to select statistically representative samples of all claims as a basis for conducting reinspections of claims by general adjusters.	Closed-Implemented
Flood Insurance: Opportunities Exist to Improve Oversight of the WYO Program: GAO-09-455, August 21, 2009	
Determine in advance the amounts built into the payment rates for estimated expenses and profit.	Open
Annually analyze the amounts of actual expenses and profit in relation to the estimated amounts used in setting payment rates.	Open
Consider the results of the analysis of payments, actual expenses, and profit in evaluating the methods for paying WYOs.	Open
Reassess the practice of paying WYOs an additional 1 percent of written premiums for operating expenses.	Open
Take actions to obtain reasonable assurance that National Association of Insurance Commissioners (NAIC) flood insurance expense data can be considered in setting payment rates that are appropriate, including identifying affiliated company profits in reported flood insurance expenses.	Open
Develop comprehensive data analysis strategies to annually test the quality of flood insurance data that WYOs report to NAIC.	Open
Improve the WYO bonus program (if FEMA continues to use this program) by considering the use of more targeted marketing goals that are in line with FEMA's NFIP goals.	Closed-Implemented
Consistently follow FEMA's Control Plan (which outlines WYO companies' responsibilities) and ensure that each component is implemented.	Closed-Implemented
Ensure that any revised Control Plan include oversight of all functions of participating WYOs, including customer service and litigation expenses.	Closed-Implemented
Systematically track insurance companies' compliance with and performance under each component of the Control Plan and ensure centralized access to all the audits, reviews, and data analyses performed for each participating insurance company under the Control Plan.	Closed-Implemented
Flood Insurance: FEMA's Rate-Setting Process Warrants Attention: GAO-09-12, October 31, 2008	
Take steps to ensure that rate-setting methods and the data it uses to set rates result in full-risk premium rates that accurately reflect the risk of losses from flooding. These steps should include, for example, verifying the accuracy of flood probabilities, damage estimates, and flood maps; ensuring that the effects of long-term planned and ongoing development, as well as climate change, are reflected in the flood probabilities used; and reevaluating the practice of aggregating risks across zones.	Open
Ensure that information is collected on the location, number, and losses associated with existing and newly created grandfathered properties in NFIP and analyze the financial impact of these properties on the flood insurance program.	Open
National Flood Insurance Programs: Financial Challenges Underscore Need for Improved Oversight of Mitigation Programs and Key Contracts: GAO-08-437, June 16, 2008.	
Ensure that FEMA staff clearly monitor each performance standard that the contractor is required to meet in the time frames required by contract and that FEMA staff clearly link monitoring reports and performance areas.	Closed-Implemented

Implement a process to ensure that monitoring reports are submitted on time and systematically reviewed by the Contracting Officer's Representative (COR) and the Program Management Office and copies of monitoring reports are retained in a quality assurance file, as directed by the contract.	Closed-Implemented
Establish a means to track real-time property acquisitions for NFIP-funded mitigation programs.	Open
Establish written guidance for FEMA regional offices to better ensure consistent and timely recording of property acquisition data.	Open
Ensure implementation of written guidance for all NFIP-related contracts on how to consistently handle the failure of a contractor to meet standards in performance areas and establish written policies and procedures about the coordination between FEMA officials and offices (including the COR, the Program Management Office, and the Contracting Officer)when addressing contractor deficiencies, including determining whether and under what circumstances to issue discrepancy reports, and ensuring that financial disincentives are appropriately and consistently applied.	Closed-Implemented

Source: GAO.

Related GAO Reports on NFIP

Extreme Weather Events: Limiting Federal Fiscal Exposure and Increasing the Nation's Resilience. GAO-14-364T. Washington, D.C.: February 12, 2014.

Flood Insurance: Strategies for Increasing Private Sector Involvement. GAO-14-127. Washington, D.C.: January 22, 2014.

National Flood Insurance Program: Progress Made on Contract Management but Monitoring and Reporting Could Be Improved. GAO-14-160. Washington, D.C.: January 15, 2014.

National Flood Insurance Program: Continued Attention Needed to Address Challenges. GAO-13-858T. Washington, D.C.: September 18, 2013.

NOAA: Initial Response to Post-Storm Assessment Requirements. GAO-13-559R. Washington, D.C.: July 11, 2013.

Flood Insurance: More Information Needed on Subsidized Properties. GAO-13-607. Washington, D.C.: July 3, 2013.

Flood Insurance: Implications of Changing Coverage Limits and Expanding Coverage. GAO-13-568. Washington, D.C.: July 3, 2013.

High-Risk Series: An Update. GAO-13-283. Washington, D.C.: February 2013.

Flood Insurance: Participation of Indian Tribes in Federal and Private Programs. GAO-13-226. Washington, D.C.: January 4, 2013.

Federal Emergency Management Agency: Workforce Planning and Training Could Be Enhanced by Incorporating Strategic Management Principles. GAO-12-487. Washington, D.C.: April 26, 2012.

FEMA and the Corps Have Taken Steps to Establish a Task Force, but FEMA Has Not Assessed the Costs of Collecting and Reporting All Levee-Related Concerns. GAO-11-689R. Washington, D.C.: July 29, 2011.

Flood Insurance: Public Policy Goals Provide A Framework for Reform. GAO-11-670T. Washington, D.C.: June 23, 2011.

FEMA: Action Needed to Improve Administration of the National Flood Insurance Program. GAO-11-297. Washington, D.C.: June 9, 2011.

Flood Insurance: Public Policy Goals Provide A Framework for Reform. GAO-11-429T. Washington, D.C.: March 11, 2011.

FEMA Flood Maps: Some Standards and Processes in Place to Promote Map Accuracy and Outreach, but Opportunities Exist to Address Implementation Challenges. GAO-11-17. Washington, D.C.: December 2, 2010.

National Flood Insurance Program: Continued Actions Needed to Address Financial and Operational Issues. GAO-10-1063T. Washington, D.C.: September 22, 2010.

National Flood Insurance Program: Continued Actions Needed to Address Financial and Operational Issues. GAO-10-631T. Washington, D.C.: April 21, 2010.

Financial Management: Improvements Needed in National Flood Insurance Program's Financial Controls and Oversight. GAO-10-66. Washington, D.C.: December 22, 2009.

Flood Insurance: Opportunities Exist to Improve Oversight of the WYO Program. GAO-09-455. Washington, D.C.: August 21, 2009.

Information on Proposed Changes to the National Flood Insurance Program. GAO-09-420R. Washington, D.C.: February 27, 2009.

Flood Insurance: Options for Addressing the Financial Impact of Subsidized Premium Rates on the National Flood Insurance Program. GAO-09-20. Washington, D.C.: November 14, 2008.

Flood Insurance: FEMA's Rate-Setting Process Warrants Attention. GAO-09-12. Washington, D.C.: October 31, 2008.

National Flood Insurance Program: Financial Challenges Underscore Need for Improved Oversight of Mitigation Programs and Key Contracts. GAO-08-437. Washington, D.C.: June 16, 2008.

Natural Catastrophe Insurance: Analysis of a Proposed Combined Federal Flood and Wind Insurance Program. GAO-08-504. Washington, D.C.: April 25, 2008.

National Flood Insurance Program: Greater Transparency and Oversight of Wind and Flood Damage Determinations Are Needed. GAO-08-28. Washington, D.C.: December 28, 2007.

Natural Disasters: Public Policy Options for Changing the Federal Role in Natural Catastrophe Insurance. GAO-08-7. Washington, D.C.: November 26, 2007.

Federal Emergency Management Agency: Ongoing Challenges Facing the National Flood Insurance Program. GAO-08-118T. Washington, D.C.: October 2, 2007.

National Flood Insurance Program: FEMA's Management and Oversight of Payments for Insurance Company Services Should Be Improved. GAO-07-1078. Washington, D.C.: September 5, 2007.

Natural Hazard Mitigation: Various Mitigation Efforts Exist, but Federal Efforts Do Not Provide a Comprehensive Strategic Framework. GAO-07-403. Washington, D.C.: August 22, 2007.

National Flood Insurance Program: Preliminary Views on FEMA's Ability to Ensure Accurate Payments on Hurricane-Damaged Properties. GAO-07-991T. Washington, D.C.: June 12, 2007.

Coastal Barrier Resources System: Status of Development That Has Occurred and Financial Assistance Provided by Federal Agencies. GAO-07-356. Washington, D.C.: March 19, 2007.

Budget Issues: FEMA Needs Adequate Data, Plans, and Systems to Effectively Manage Resources for Day-to-Day Operations. GAO-07-139. Washington, D.C.: January 19, 2007.

National Flood Insurance Program: New Processes Aided Hurricane Katrina Claims Handling, but FEMA's Oversight Should Be Improved. GAO-07-169. Washington, D.C.: December 15, 2006.

GAO's High-Risk Program. GAO-06-497T. Washington, D.C.: March 15, 2006.

Federal Emergency Management Agency: Challenges for the National Flood Insurance Program. GAO-06-335T. Washington, D.C.: January 25, 2006.

Federal Emergency Management Agency: Improvements Needed to Enhance Oversight and Management of the National Flood Insurance Program. GAO-06-119. Washington, D.C.: October 18, 2005.

Federal Emergency Management Agency: Challenges Facing the National Flood Insurance Program. GAO-06-174T. Washington, D.C.: October 18, 2005.

Flood Map Modernization: Federal Emergency Management Agency's Implementation of a National Strategy. GAO-05-894T (Washington, D.C.: July 12, 2005).

National Flood Insurance Program: Oversight of Policy Issuance and Claims. GAO-05-532T. Washington, D.C.: April 14, 2005.

Flood Map Modernization: Program Strategy Shows Promise, but Challenges Remain. GAO-04-417. Washington, D.C.: March 31, 2004.

National Flood Insurance Program: Actions to Address Repetitive Loss Properties. GAO-04-401T. Washington, D.C.: March 25, 2004.

Flood Insurance: Challenges Facing the National Flood Insurance Program. GAO-03-606T. Washington, D.C.: April 1, 2003.

(250747)

GAO's Mission	The Government Accountability Office, the audit, evaluation, and investigative arm of Congress, exists to support Congress in meeting its constitutional responsibilities and to help improve the performance and accountability of the federal government for the American people. GAO examines the use of public funds; evaluates federal programs and policies; and provides analyses, recommendations, and other assistance to help Congress make informed oversight, policy, and funding decisions. GAO's commitment to good government is reflected in its core values of accountability, integrity, and reliability.
Obtaining Copies of GAO Reports and Testimony	The fastest and easiest way to obtain copies of GAO documents at no cost is through GAO's website (www.gao.gov). Each weekday afternoon, GAO posts on its website newly released reports, testimony, and correspondence. To have GAO e-mail you a list of newly posted products, go to www.gao.gov and select "E-mail Updates."
Order by Phone	The price of each GAO publication reflects GAO's actual cost of production and distribution and depends on the number of pages in the publication and whether the publication is printed in color or black and white. Pricing and ordering information is posted on GAO's website, http://www.gao.gov/ordering.htm. Place orders by calling (202) 512-6000, toll free (866) 801-7077, or TDD (202) 512-2537. Orders may be paid for using American Express, Discover Card, MasterCard, Visa, check, or money order. Call for additional information.
Connect with GAO	Connect with GAO on Facebook, Flickr, Twitter, and YouTube. Subscribe to our RSS Feeds or E-mail Updates. Listen to our Podcasts. Visit GAO on the web at www.gao.gov.
To Report Fraud, Waste, and Abuse in Federal Programs	Contact: Website: www.gao.gov/fraudnet/fraudnet.htm E-mail: fraudnet@gao.gov Automated answering system: (800) 424-5454 or (202) 512-7470
Congressional Relations	Katherine Siggerud, Managing Director, siggerudk@gao.gov, (202) 512-4400, U.S. Government Accountability Office, 441 G Street NW, Room 7125, Washington, DC 20548
Public Affairs	Chuck Young, Managing Director, youngc1@gao.gov, (202) 512-4800 U.S. Government Accountability Office, 441 G Street NW, Room 7149 Washington, DC 20548

www.ingramcontent.com/pod-product-compliance
Lightning Source LLC
Chambersburg PA
CBHW080543290526
45790CB00006B/2531